OLD TESTAME

General E
R.N. Whybray

RUTH AND ESTHER

RUTH AND ESTHER

Katrina J.A. Larkin

Sheffield Academic Press

Published by Sheffield Academic Press Ltd
Mansion House
19 Kingfield Road
Sheffield, S11 9AS
England

Printed on acid-free paper in Great Britain
by The Cromwell Press
Melksham, Wiltshire

British Library Cataloguing in Publication Data

A catalogue record for this book is available
from the British Library

ISBN 1-85075-755-0

Contents

Preface

Since I believe that the book of Ruth is often used as a set text by students of biblical Hebrew, that part of this Guide which deals with the book of Ruth is written with the needs of such students in mind. It is, however, also intended to be comprehensible to the general reader, and it will be found that the few Hebrew words which do appear are all translated as they occur.

I am grateful to have been given the opportunity of preparing this volume, particularly as it deals with the only two biblical books to have been named after women. I dedicate it to my mother, Lydia Isabel Swan, who is a born story-teller in the best oral tradition.

Katrina Larkin
King's College, London
June 1995

Abbreviations

AB	Anchor Bible
ATD	Das Alte Testament Deutsch
BA	*Biblical Archaeologist*
BARev	*Biblical Archaeological Review*
Bib	*Biblica*
BKAT	Biblische Kommentar zum Alten Testament
BTB	Biblical Theology Bulletin
CBQ	*Catholic Biblical Quarterly*
HAR	*Hebrew Annual Review*
HTR	*Harvard Theological Review*
HUCA	*Hebrew Union College Annual*
ICC	International Critical Commentary
ITC	International Theological Commentary
JBL	*Journal of Biblical Literature*
JJS	*Journal of Jewish Studies*
JR	*Journal of Religion*
JSOT	*Journal for the Study of the Old Testament*
KAT	Kommentar zum Alten Testament
NCB	New Century Bible Commentary
NEB	New English Bible
NIB	New International Bible Commentary
NRSV	New Revised Standard Version
RB	*Revue Biblique*
RevQ	*Revue de Qumran*
RTR	*Reformed Theological Review*
SBLDS	Society of Biblical Literature Dissertation Series
SBLMS	Society of Biblical Literature Monograph Series
SBM	Stuttgarter Biblische Monographien
SEÅ	*Svensk Exegetisk Årsbok*
TynBul	*Tyndale Bulletin*
TZ	*Theologische Zeitschrift*
UBS	United Bible Societies (Monograph Series)
VT	*Vetus Testamentum*
ZAW	*Zeitschrift für die Alttestamentlicher Wissenschaft*

1

INTRODUCTION

THE POWER OF A GOOD STORY lies in its capacity to speak to the whole person—imagination, memory, affectivity and reason. A story becomes great when it transcends the boundaries of the place and time of its first telling, and proves not to be limited to a particular historical context. It can be argued that we have two such stories in the books of Ruth and Esther (so, for example, Carmel McCarthy in *The Hebrew Short Story*). Here we have two books distinguished as being the only two canonical books named after women, and this leads us to expect that in each case the woman should be either the heroine or writer of the story. In both cases inspection of the contents shows that the woman is the heroine.

To be more precise, both books might be classified as novellas or 'short stories'. Such classification is significant theologically because a basic assumption of literary criticism is that similar texts (texts belonging to the same genre) reflect and respond to similar needs and interests, so that to know the genre of a text is to know something of the author's purposes and strategies, and something of the way in which the original audience was supposed to respond to it. Of course, the genre 'short story' is still quite a wide category that raises fairly simple expectations such as that it is written by a single author and meant to be read rather than recited. Typically, it sketches a tense situation, introduces a number of complicating factors, and finally produces a resolution; it will be self-contained, and more interested in characters and plot development than in reporting historical events.

There is some disagreement about how far back this broad genre can be traced, and whether it may even have appeared first in Hebrew tradition; the answer to this question partly depends on what range of differences can be tolerated among early exemplars assigned to the same category. The argument is complicated by the fact that no text is wholly pure in genre but rather belongs to a number of overlapping or nesting sets (so Fox in his *Character and Ideology in the Book of Esther*); nor does careful study support the expectation of early modern scholars such as Gunkel—often called the father of modern Ruth studies—that genres at least begin pure even if they degenerate subsequently.

This area of doubt over the origins and development of the short story genre is further compounded by the difficulty of dating certain key examples, such as the book of Ruth. On one view the antecedents of Ruth can be sought in very ancient material stemming from the local fertility cults of Canaan and/or Egyptian tales, worked over in the reign of Solomon, and brought into the present form in the post-exilic period. The book is then said to be of similar genre to admittedly shorter (and not free-standing) biblical prose tales such as the story of Tamar in Genesis 38, individual story units in Judges, the prose frame of Job, or the Court History of 2 Samuel 9–20 (notice how such comparisons imply that there is no boundary which clearly divides fiction from historical narrative!).

The book of Esther is more often compared to such obviously late material as the story cycle in Daniel 1–6, or to the apocryphal stories of Judith and Tobit. Yet occasionally Ruth and Esther are compared to each other, either directly or more often indirectly through a shared comparison with the Joseph story (a discontinuous narrative in Gen. 37–50), a story whose own date and provenance—and hence its chronological place in the Ruth, Esther, Joseph triumvirate—is uncertain and problematic.

It can only be said that Esther is likely to be the most recent of the three, as it cannot be older than the Persian period in which it is set, even if, like Ruth, it is sometimes alleged (and with greater reason) to have ancient roots which are partly pagan.

Thematically, what all these three stories have in common is that all are literature born of enforced residence in an alien land. All of them bring together Israelite and foreign cultures, and between them they show a range of different attitudes in Israel to foreigners, united by the common insistence that meaningful human relations are possible across national barriers and even that the Lord works to bring them about. The same theme is found in other late texts such as Daniel 1–6 and the apocryphal book of Judith. Ruth stands somewhat apart from the others, however, in picturing a foreigner among Jews, rather than Jews among foreigners. These stories are also alike in that in each case the problems addressed by the storyteller affect many more people than the named protagonists: in Ruth, the action of the story perpetuates a family line that might have died out, yet was saved through the marriage of Ruth and Boaz to produce—three generations later—the great king David. In Joseph the survival of the tribal fathers of all Israel is at stake; and in Esther the survival of all the Jews of the Persian diaspora.

The three stories are all concerned with the outworking of God's providence, and assume either implicitly (Esther) or explicitly (Ruth; and especially Joseph) that the divine all-causality is hidden in the working of normal causality. There are no overt miracles in any of these books. In neither Ruth nor Esther can people necessarily 'read' events aright as they occur, even though they are bound to take action as best they can in faithfulness to God and to one another. Events will show that faithfulness is related to reward, and a 'reversal of fortune' pattern is evident in each one, yet no mechanical doctrine of reward and punishment is put forward at all. Joseph tackles this theme with some didacticism (possibly because it has a closer wisdom influence in its background than the other two); Ruth is much more allusive in its handling of the theme of hidden providence; and Esther notoriously avoids mentioning God or any of Israel's laws or cultic institutions at all. Indeed Hals in his *Theology of the Book of Ruth* says that this trait in Esther is a *reductio ad absurdum* of the reticence of Ruth on such matters. Both Ruth and Esther are concerned with the right handling of law-based authority.

Naturally the comparisons become more tenuous the more closely one looks. Ruth and Esther are indeed similar in their use of history-like detail, and in the use of literary devices such as irony, wordplay, foreshadowing and anticipation, and coincidences as plot devices. A motif of obtaining food is present in both, and in each there is an association of a principal character with the city 'gate' (Mordecai in Est. 2.19; Boaz in Ruth 4.1). But Ruth breathes a calmness which is reflected in its very symmetrical and artistic structure, while Esther is full of fear, bloodshed and harsh dualisms, even containing numerous examples of 'twoness' in its composition. There are no linguistic correspondences between the two books, although some have been found between Esther and Joseph.

In the best Jewish tradition it appears that both Ruth and Esther belong to the third division of the Hebrew Bible known as the Writings (though this is controversial in the case of Ruth, as will be seen), placing Ruth first in a presumed chronological order of authorship and Esther last of all.

In the Christian canon, Ruth is placed after Judges partly because a Hellenized canonical tradition is appealed to, and partly because the book is set in the period of the judges; and Esther is placed after the histories of Ezra and Nehemiah, again as it is set in the Persian period to which those histories relate. But the historicity of both books has come under serious fire from modern scholars. As will appear, the existence of a historical core is still defended by some scholars for each book: the fact that David had a Moabite great-grandmother may underlie Ruth; and the existence of some real threat to the existence of Jews in the Persian diaspora may underlie Esther (although in the case of Esther it is harder to determine what the historical core might be, it has often been assumed that some such event as a pogrom must have occurred to justify the adoption by all Jews of the feast of Purim).

In the Jewish tradition, Esther and Ruth are not merely alike in belonging to the Writings but also in belonging to the smaller collection of Megilloth, five scrolls with special status as selected readings for use at major festivals (the other three are the Song of Songs, Ecclesiastes and Lamentations). Ruth may either be placed first of the five—the order found in most printed Hebrew Bibles—so that it follows Proverbs which ends with a poem in praise of a 'worthy woman'; or the books can be given in order of the festivals to which they relate, beginning with the Song of Songs for Passover, continuing with Ruth as the reading for Shabu'ot (the Feast of Weeks marking the harvest festival of the first-fruits, and equivalent to Pentecost in the Christian calendar), and ending with Esther, for reading at the feast of Purim on the 14th-15th Adar (in February–March), a festival which has no Christian equivalent but which celebrates national deliverance and victory by the Jews over their enemies.

The festival connection is much stronger in the case of Esther than of Ruth. Ruth seems to be connected to Shabu'ot purely because the action centres on the time of the barley harvest which the feast celebrates, although the feast itself is nowhere mentioned explicitly. Esther by contrast could be classified as a festal legend or aetiology, as it purports to explain the origins of the festival of Purim (which is not mentioned in the Mosaic laws of the Pentateuch), and is the only biblical text which enjoins the observance of the festival.

Despite the latter, which probably was an obstacle to the acceptance of Esther into the Jewish canon, it is in fact this very popular festival connection which ultimately seems to have gained Esther its place within the canon. Unlike the book of Ruth, Esther has always evoked very mixed and sometimes hostile reactions. It is vulnerable to attack not only on the ground of its lateness but also because of its lack of overt religiosity and its vengeful ending with the death of over 75,000 Gentiles. On these grounds the rabbis were reluctant to admit it to the canon, and despite a readiness on the part of the Council of Jamnia to accept it in the first century, protests against it continued until the fourth century ad. Christians, with no reason to appreciate the festival connection (rather the contrary!) have historically been even less enthusiastic, although in recent scholarship the two traditions have both reassessed their attitudes, with potentially fruitful results.

A significant new line of scholarship in relation to both

books concerns their feminist significance. For example, both Ruth and Esther have been compared and contrasted with the 'deceptive goddesses' of neighbouring cultures who frequently appear in contexts which include motifs of sexual exchange, drunkenness, and feasting (Ruth 3; Est. 5.4-8). Possibly neither was written by a woman, although Campbell in his commentary on Ruth suggests it as a possibility that 'wise women' or alternatively Levites were responsible for its first telling. So far as the characters of the heroines are concerned, Esther has had a very mixed press from feminists: she accepts life in the harem (which her predecessor as queen, Vashti, had repudiated with some spirit), and essentially obeys Mordecai as the plot unfolds; moreover, the book that bears her name seems to run counter to feminist values in its repeated portrayals of disharmony and ultimately bloodshed on a grand scale. But do we not have to take the story on its own cultural terms, in which to disobey is to court death? It is Esther's very lack of power that makes her a paradigm of the diaspora Jew (so Sidnie White).

More surprisingly, some feminists are equally wary of Ruth as a role model: she too, it is said, finds fulfilment in submission and obedience, and the point of including her story in the Bible is to fill in a gap in the patriarchal hierarchy leading up to the begetting of David. Yet Meyer (in the *Feminist Companion to Ruth*) sees the book of Ruth as a rare window into the positive reality of women's lives in the Old Testament period, and it is true that the book does make wonderful use of symbols that are arguably feminine: peace, plenty, progeny, all portrayed against the background of the gathering in of the barley harvest. And both Ruth and Esther need courage, resourcefulness and subtlety to play their parts in the outworking of God's salvation. Both stories are subversive of rigid adherence to imperfect norms by showing how two disadvantaged foreigners deconstruct gender boundaries in order to save themselves and others.

In this connection it is worth pausing to consider as McCarthy does just how stories function theologically. Laws and prophetic warnings seem easier to interpret because they give express commands to be obeyed, whereas a storyteller first and foremost wishes to captivate and hold an audience. But a *truthful* story may have distinct theological advantages over abstract thought and concepts which most people do not find absorbing. It can present facets of reality which we are unwilling to acknowledge as such in theory; it takes root in the mind and stimulates growth of a kind that will vary from person to person. These are points to bear in mind in attempting to establish the theological function of the stories of Ruth and Esther.

For Further Reading

R. Alter and F. Kermode (eds.), *The Literary Guide to the Bible* (Cambridge, MA: Harvard University Press, 1987), pp. 320-28, 335-42.

A.O. Bellis, *Helpmates, Harlots, Heroes: Women's Stories in the Hebrew Bible* (Louisville, KY: Westminster; 1994), pp. 206-26 (reviews feminist scholarship).

Katheryn Pfister Darr, *Far More Precious Than Jewels: Perspectives on Biblical Women* (Louisville: Westminster/John Knox Press, 1991).

Carmel McCarthy and William Riley, *The Old Testament Short Story: Explorations into Narrative Spirituality* (Message of Biblical Spirituality, 7; Wilmington, DE: Michael Glazier, 1986), pp. 55-83, 84-111.

S. Niditch, 'Legends of Wise Heroes and Heroines', in *The Hebrew Bible and Its Modern Interpreters* (ed. D.A. Knight and G.M. Tucker; Philadelphia: Fortress Press, 1985), pp. 445-63.

Among commentaries on Ruth those by Gray, Hubbard and Campbell are very accessible (Hubbard has a preference for conservative options). Sasson's philological commentary may look forbidding at first sight but will be valuable to those studying the Hebrew text and is more up-to-date than the comparable work by Joüon. Zenger is very concise, and Rudolph a good example of sensitive historical criticism. Gerleman has also written a commentary on Esther.

E.F. Campbell, *Ruth* (AB; Garden City NY: Doubleday, 1975).

G. Gerleman, *Ruth* (BK, 17; Neukirchen–Vluyn: Neukirchener Verlag, 1965).

J. Gray, *Joshua, Judges, Ruth* (NCB; Grand Rapids: Eerdmans, 1986).

R.L. Hubbard, *The Book of Ruth* (NIC, 14; Grand Rapids: Eerdmans, 1988).

P. Joüon, *Ruth: commentaire philologique et exegetique* (Rome: Pontifical Biblical Institute, 1953).

W. Rudolph, *Das Buch Ruth* (KAT, 17.1; Gütersloh: Mohn, 2nd edn, 1962).

J.M. Sasson, *Ruth: A New Translation with a Philological Commentary and a Formalist-Folklorist Interpretation* (Sheffield: JSOT Press, 2nd edn, 1989).

E. Zenger, *Das Buch Ruth* (Zürcher Bibelkommentar; Zürich: Theologischer Verlag, 1986).

Other useful monographs or collections on Ruth include:

A. Brenner (ed.), *A Feminist Companion to Ruth* (Feminist Companion to the Bible, 3; Sheffield: JSOT Press, 1993).

M. Gow, *The Book of Ruth: Its Structure, Theme and Purpose* (Leicester: Apollos, 1992). (On the original intention and continuing function of the book).

Commentaries on Esther include:

H. Bardtke, *Das Buch Esther* (KAT, 17.5; Gütersloh: Gerd Mohn, 1963).

D.J.A. Clines, *Ezra, Nehemiah, Esther* (NCB; Grand Rapids: Eerdmans, 1984). Fresh and succinct.

M.V. Fox, *Character and Ideology in the Book of Esther* (Studies on Personalities of the Old Testament; Columbia: University of South Carolina Press, 1991). Contains all the ingredients of a commentary as well as the character studies specified in the title.

G. Gerleman, *Esther* (BKAT, 21; Neukirchen–Vluyn: Neukirchener Verlag, 1973).

R. Gordis, *Megillat Esther: The Masoretic Hebrew Text with Introduction, New Translation and Commentary* (New York: Ktav, 1974).

A. Meinhold, *Das Buch Esther* (Zürcher Bibelkommentare, AT 13; Zürich: Theologischer Verlag, 1983).

C.A. Moore, *Esther: Introduction, Translation and Notes* (AB, 7B; New York: Doubleday, 1971).

—*Daniel, Esther and Jeremiah: The Additions* (AB, 44; New York: Doubleday, 1977), pp. 153-252.

—*Studies in the Book of Esther* (New York: Ktav, 1982).

L.B. Paton, *The Book of Esther* (ICC; Edinburgh: T. & T. Clark, 1908).

S.P. Re'emi, *Esther* (ITC; Grand Rapids and Edinburgh: Eerdmans, 1985).

Other useful monographs or collections on Esther include:

S.B. Berg, *The Book of Esther: Motifs, Themes, Structures* (SBLDS, 44; Chico: Scholars Press, 1979).

A. Brenner (ed.), *A Feminist Companion to Esther, Judith and Susanna* (Feminist Companion to the Bible, 7; Sheffield: JSOT Press, 1995), pp.1-206.

D.J.A. Clines, *The Esther Scroll: The Story of the Story* (JSOTSup, 30; Sheffield: JSOT Press, 1984).

Ruth

2

RUTH
THE PROBLEM OF DATE

THE TRADITIONAL JEWISH VIEW of the authorship of Ruth as recorded in the Babylonian Talmud (*Baba Bathra* 14b-15a) is that it was written by the prophet Samuel. This, however, is most unlikely, even on the internal evidence of the Bible itself which is that Samuel had died some time before David—whom the genealogies in 4.17, 18-22 presume to be well known—had become king. The opening words 'And it came to pass in the days when the judges judged...' (translated by the NEB as 'Long ago...') may already distance the content from the reader, and 4.7 'Now this was the custom in former times in Israel...'(explaining a legal custom which has fallen into disuse) has the same effect. Consequently it has long been thought that the tale is in fact later than the time in which it is set, subject to the proviso that the genealogies may be secondary to the story proper. Wellhausen believed the whole book to be late.

The outer limits for dating the book must begin with the reign of David, because of the subject matter, and end with the acceptance of the book into the canon in the mid-second century BC. In practice, scholars divide into two broad groups: those who believe the book to be pre-exilic and those who believe it to be post-exilic. There is very little support for the view that it dates from the exilic period, although the idea is not unknown.

The question of the dating of Ruth has never been satisfactorily resolved since there are no conclusive arguments, and indeed scholars reach opposite conclusions from the very same bodies of evidence; but the majority view in this century has been that it is post-exilic (fifth to fourth century) in its present form. The arguments fall into two loose categories, those which appeal to evidence internal to the book, and those which attempt to place the book in its most plausible historical, literary or theological context.

Arguments from Internal Evidence

The Dating of the Hebrew

The book has been alleged to contain a number of late linguistic forms, including Aramaisms. The significance of the latter point is that Aramaic began to supplant Hebrew as the common language of Israel from the Babylonian period onward and its presence thus points to a post-exilic dating. But the alleged number of Aramaisms in Ruth has on closer inspection been reduced to almost nil: a definitive Aramaic lexicon produced by Wagner in 1966 regards only two verb forms in 1.13 as 'more or less certain' to be Aramaic (*śābar*, Piel, 'to wait'; *ʿāgan*, Niphal, 'to be chained'), and recognizes no Aramaic grammatical constructions in Ruth, while Sasson in his philological commentary denies that even these two verbs are Aramaic. It can also be objected that although it is true that the use of Aramaic increased at a late date, its influence began early (see for example the incident recorded in 2 Kgs 18.17-37 from 701 BC), so that a small amount is quite compatible with an early date.

Similar problems surround the identification of late Hebrew forms. For example the idiom *nāśʾa ʾiššāh* for 'take a wife' in 1.4 is supposed to be later than the more normal *lāqaḥ ʾiššāh*, but is also found in Judg. 21.23; *mᵃrgelōt* 'place of feet' (3.4) is only otherwise found in Dan. 10.6, yet it is not clear how significant this is when the antonym *mᵉraᵡᵃšōt* 'place of head' is found in Gen. 28.11, 18. To complicate matters further, it is entirely possible that some of the grammatical constructions in Ruth actually follow a northern dialect which would in principle be difficult to date. The major feature of this kind is the occurrence seven times of a masculine plural suffix with feminine plural antecedents;

since there are always two women involved in these cases, it is likely that the supposedly masculine suffixes are really dual suffixes which are dialectal.

It may seem extraordinary that alongside these arguments concerning the alleged lateness of the language is another raft of arguments that there are early linguistic features in Ruth. Most of the names can be shown to be Canaanite and also appear in Ugaritic texts. There are some other arguably archaic items of vocabulary such as the old term *y^ebimah* for 'sister' (1.15); 'Shaddai' for God (1.20-21); and a possibly archaic divine epithet *m^e'ōd* (1.13). The term for 'country' is used three times with the usual orthography (1.6; 2.6; 4.3) but four times with unusual and possibly ancient orthography (1.1, 2, 6, 22). There are some unusual verb forms, six with the 'paragogic nun',[1] and some allegedly classical turns of phrase.

But the significance of all such items is arguable: for example, Sasson reckons the paragogic nun to be known to all phases of biblical Hebrew. There are a few words and idioms in Ruth which are found nowhere else in the Old Testament and whose significance in terms of date is wholly opaque. Overall, therefore, the linguistic arguments for an early date have proved as unconvincing as those for a late date. Insofar as the unusual forms, whether described as 'Aramaic' or 'archaic' may be dialectal, it is almost impossible to tell what their implications are for date.

Some scholars do feel able to draw tentative conclusions from the linguistic evidence (Hubbard believing that on balance it favours an early date, and Gordis a late one, for example). One could also say that the very inconsistency of the evidence might point to a long period of transmission before the story reached its present form. But overall it should be accepted that there are two major problems with this whole line of enquiry, namely (1) that the evidence is so inconsistent; and (2) that really we have too small a corpus of extra-biblical Hebrew vocabulary from which to draw comparisons (Sasson). The line of enquiry is probably better abandoned.

1. An additional 'n' at the end of the word.

References to Biblical Law

The book of Ruth alludes to Israelite law in several respects, but does not always square with it. I have already mentioned the explanation given in 4.7 of a shoe ceremony apparently related to Deut. 25.9 but no longer understood. More seriously, the law of levirate marriage (the arrangement whereby the brother or other close male relative of a deceased man marries the man's widow and raises children in the deceased's name), a law set out in Deut. 25.5-10, is alluded to but not strictly followed; Ruth seems either to broaden or misinterpret Deuteronomy. On the other hand, the book does contain a parade example of Deut. 24.19-22 at work, making provision (of a sort) at harvest time for 'the alien, the orphan and the widow' (compare Lev. 19.1-10; 23.22).

On this basis it is often assumed that the story must post-date the relevant legal codes by some time, and since Deuteronomy 12–26 arguably dates from the seventh century, the Holiness Code of Leviticus 17–26 from the early sixth century and the Priestly laws from the exile, Ruth must be post-exilic. But suspicions about this line of argument are immediately raised when one sees that it can be turned around: perhaps Ruth predates Deut. 25.9 and the prohibition on mixed marriages in Deut. 23.4; perhaps it reflects the general *gōʾēl* or redeemer tradition (whereby someone, usually a next-of-kin, acts to keep intact the property and name of a family) rather than the specifically levirate tradition which overlaps with it. Perhaps the shoe custom in Deut. 25.9 is not the same as that in Ruth, but has a different emphasis; and although it is true that 4.7 suggests that the writer is looking back to a past time when symbolic acts took the place of legal documentation, it is still possible to argue that the text is pre-exilic (Rudolph), but that it is seventh century rather than tenth century, and that the author is distanced from the events he describes only by the disruption caused by the introduction of the monarchy and the consequent codification of laws. Consequently, it is increasingly coming to be realized that arguments from comparative law are almost as misdirected as those from linguistic evidence.

Arguments from External Evidence

Presumed Historical Context

A favourite argument of those who believe in a post-exilic dating for Ruth appeals to the book's positive attitude towards Moab, to the extent of applauding a mixed marriage between an Israelite and a Moabite. To set this in context it should be understood that Moab (and Ammon) were traditionally—and polemically—supposed to be the fruits of Lot's incest with his daughters (Gen. 19), and that Moab was a close and frequently difficult neighbour of Israel, home of Balak who was sent to curse Israel (Num. 22–24) and a frequent foe in the days of Saul (1 Sam. 14.47)—but also a place to which David fled for protection, and sent his parents for safety. Though at one point incorporated into the Davidic kingdom (2 Sam. 8.2) the Moabites broke free in the reign of Ahab's son Ahaziah (2 Kgs 3.4-5) and were thereafter a thorn in Israel's side for the rest of the monarchical period. Thus Deut. 23.3 says that 'no Ammonite or Moabite shall enter the assembly of the Lord even to the tenth generation'. Against this background it is significant that Ruth the Moabitess embraces the people and religion of Israel as her own and is embraced by them, becoming the great-grandmother of David.

Consequently it has been suggested that Ruth dates from a tranquil period between the reforms of Ezra and Nehemiah on the one hand, and the conquests of Alexander on the other (i.e. late fifth to mid-fourth century BC), when Moab was no longer an enemy, but when the prohibitions on mixed marriages imposed by Ezra and Nehemiah (Ezra 9–10; Neh. 13.23-29) were attracting some resistance.

It is of course possible to argue about the appropriateness of this historical setting, and fair to object that the book has no polemical tone, although the proposal by Goulder that the book contains Second Temple preaching on a piece of misunderstood law could fit this setting without requiring a polemical tone. Hubbard, a recent strong supporter of the pre-exilic dating, argues that the lack of animosity to Moab is actually evidence of an early date (cf. 1 Sam. 22.3-4) and that the book's serenity could make it unlikely that it comes from post-exilic times, when life was harsh even in peacetime. It will be clear how subjective such judgments must be. There is no agreement about the real import of the Moab connection, save a commonly voiced opinion that it may be a historical datum that David had part-Moabite ancestry, since no-one would have wished to invent it otherwise. Even this, however, is challenged by Sasson on the ground that Ruth is folkloristic, and it is a requirement of the genre that the heroine go on a hazardous journey before undertaking the difficult tasks assigned to her; from this perspective, Moab is just a conveniently close foreign country.

Literary and Theological Context

Ruth is commonly accepted as an example of the Hebrew short story form, and thus compared to one of two main rafts of stories, namely those found in late biblical books such as Esther, Daniel 1–6, Jonah, and the Joseph story (?); or the earlier stories in the J and E strands of the Pentateuch and in the Deuteronomistic History, again possibly including Joseph. The story of Judah and Tamar in Genesis 38 contains some clear thematic parallels. Meinhold, on a somewhat different tack, draws comparisons between the content of Ruth and the content of Psalm 132, suggesting that both come from Bethlehem in pre-deuteronomistic times. Another particular comparison with the prose frame of Job is said to be the use of the complaint form by Naomi (Ruth 1.11-13, 20-21), which would point to a later date.

In more theological terms, Ruth is said to have a universalism and humaneness about it which set it alongside works such as Ecclesiastes and Jonah theologically, and make it late and compatible with the wisdom tradition. And its reference to 'judges' in 1.1 arguably suggests that it must be late because its author knows the Deuteronomic edition of Judges (c. 550 BC) which established the use of the term for the pre-monarchical period.

We have already noted that there are indeed comparisons to be drawn between Ruth and the later Esther but that there are also contrasts between the two. It can be argued that all of the indubitably 'late' works take place in foreign capitals in contrast with Ruth which is the only one to deal with a foreigner among Israelites, not *vice versa*. And it is fair to say that the overall perspective of Ruth is very different from that of Ecclesiastes or Jonah.

Here again, a line of argument has been produced that can yield very different results depending on where one starts. It is interesting, however, that those scholars who have fairly recently produced commentaries on Ruth tend to gravitate towards early datings, such as the Davidic or Solomonic eras. The 'Solomonic Enlightenment' is then said to have provided the background for the theological perspective which is fascinated by the hiddenness of the ways in which God's purpose is worked out in and through ordinary events and ordinary people. This was also the era in which David's simple antecedents could be accepted for what they were, before incipient messianism took over the Israelite kingly ideal (Gerleman).

But how much do we really know about the so-called 'Solomonic Enlightenment'? Many scholars would hesitate to insist that 'hidden causality' or universalistic theology is diagnostic of a particular period, even if the historicity of the Solomonic era were less uncertain than it currently appears to be. Similarly, the dating of many of the texts appealed to as literary parallels from this era is increasingly uncertain. Porten, who in 1976 found no less than fifteen parallels between Ruth and Genesis drew no historical conclusions from his findings, owing to the difficulty of dating any of this literature. Sasson rightly objects that opinions on the dating of Ruth that are formulated by establishing the context that would best explain its presence in the canon are 'not without a manifest tendency to reason circularly'.

The Canonical Context

A final and important point is that Ruth is located in the third division of the Hebrew Bible, the Writings, rather than in the Prophets, suggesting that it is too late to have been included among the Prophets. The argument is not clear-cut, in that Hellenized Jewish tradition (underlying the Septuagint canon) has placed Ruth after Judges, and in any event there are elements among the Writings that are ancient (such as certain Psalms). But it is generally accepted that the three divisions of the Hebrew Bible are in broadly chronological order, and the Talmudic tradition is clear that in the Writings Ruth comes (again in presumed chronological order) at the beginning, before the Psalms. This is surely a serious consideration which prevents the easy allocation of Ruth to a pre-exilic date.

Conclusions

It will be clear from the foregoing that neither the internal nor the external evidence for the dating of Ruth is really very compelling, and most scholars are correspondingly guarded in their conclusions. The scholar who has probably done most to insist on a pre-exilic dating is Hubbard, although Sasson is also able to envisage a late monarchical setting in which the story functioned (as folktales often do) to rally a fragmented society to its lost ideals. Von Rad, Hals, Gerleman, Beattie and Niditch also opt for pre-exilic datings. A more qualified position is that of Campbell and Rudolph, who argue (independently) that the text was first written in the Solomonic period but was edited after the exile. A post-exilic date is favoured by Gordis and Lacocque.

Notwithstanding that the story may have ancient roots extending back even behind its written form, there are hints of lateness about it which are hard to ignore. It is hardly credible to suppose that the story has not been touched since the time of Solomon.

For Further Reading

E.F. Campbell, 'The Hebrew Short Story: A Study of Ruth', in H.N. Bream (ed.), *A Light Unto My Path, fs. JM Myers* (Gettysburg Theological Studies, 4; Gettysburg: Temple University Press, 1974), pp. 83-101.

G.S. Glanzman, 'The Origin and Date of the Book of Ruth', *CBQ* 21 (1959), pp. 201-207.

M. Goulder, 'Ruth, a Homily on Deuteronomy 22-25?', in H.A. McKay and D.J.A. Clines (eds.), *Of Prophet's Visions and the Wisdom of Sages. Essays in Honour of R. Norman Whybray on his Seventieth Birthday* (JSOTSup, 162; Sheffield: JSOT Press, 1993), pp. 307-19.

R.M. Hals, *The Theology of the Book of Ruth* (Philadelphia: Fortress Press, 1969).

A. Lacocque, 'Date et milieu du livre de Ruth', *Revue d'histoire et de Philosophie Réligieuse* 59 (1979), pp. 583-93.

A. Meinhold, 'Theologische Schwerpunkte im Buch Ruth und ihr Schwergewicht für seine Datierung', *TZ* 32 (1976), pp. 129-37.

Jean-Luc Vesco, 'La date du livre de Ruth', *RB* 74 (1967), pp. 235-47.

3

RUTH
THE LEGAL BACKGROUND

WHETHER OR NOT the attitude to law shown in Ruth has to do with the purpose of the book (as not only those who date it early but also Goulder would say that it does), it is still true that the issue is an important one which needs to be investigated. The genealogy of Perez which concludes the book (4.18-22) is that of a clan of Judah which was partly Canaanite, with Perez himself being the son of Judah and his daughter-in-law Tamar, whose union was of the levirate type. The genealogy thus establishes the fact that two marriages of levirate or similar type occurred in the ancestry of David, and thus of Jesus.

Ruth alludes to a number of features of Israelite law, sometimes in a problematic manner, and this is most true of the laws governing levirate marriage and redemption. Levirate marriage is literally 'brother-in-law marriage' (from the Latin *levir*, 'husband's brother') and is governed by Deut. 25.5-10. It is the arrangement whereby a close male relative of a dead man will marry the widow to raise children to inherit the property in the dead man's name. This at first fails to work for Ruth, as Naomi has 'no more sons' (1.8-14). The duty of redemption is somewhat different, though related. Governed by Lev. 25.23-24, 47-55, it covers the situation in which an Israelite has to sell his inheritance (or himself into slavery) to pay debts; in that case, it is the duty of the next of kin to keep the property and the name of the family intact by acting as buyer-back or redeemer, *gōʾēl*, if possible (the property aspect of this law can be seen at work in Jer. 32.6-12). Allusions to these arrangements appear in Ruth 2.20; 3.9, 12-13; and 4.4, 6. The unnamed man of Ruth 4.1 is Naomi's *gō'ēl*, and Boaz is apparently next in line. What is not clear is how Ruth herself enters in. The text suggests that the *gō'ēl* has to have her as well as Naomi's field, get children by her, and allow them to inherit the property (4.3-5). But this is an unusual combination, found only here, and the next-of-kin refuses on the ground that it would damage his own inheritance (4.6). What is the reason for this confusion?

Among those who regard these details as essentially correct—neither a late misunderstanding of older laws, nor a critical response to those laws—the discussion of Hubbard (pp. 48-63) is particularly full and accessible. This line of approach entails arguing that we can in fact deduce otherwise unknown information about Israel's legal system from the book of Ruth, even if the 'problem' is partly just a manifestation of the gap that inevitably arises between 'policy' (the establishment of agreed legal norms) and 'technique', the application of policy to specific and perhaps unique cases. It is relatively easy to argue that Ruth shows that it was part of the broad duty of a *gō'ēl* to marry a widow if need be, even though Deuteronomy 25 does not specifically say that it was. The other problems that arise are much more thorny, if one wishes to maintain a historicizing viewpoint. Briefly, they are as follows.

First, it is strange that in 4.3 we suddenly hear that Naomi is selling a piece of Elimelech's property. This is totally unexpected when the two women have been shown living such a precarious life at Bethlehem, gleaning in order to survive. If this is not just a storyteller's device, it has to be postulated that a widow could inherit property in Israel, if only on trust pending its disposal to a male heir, and that in practice changes in the user of the land were left to be resolved after the harvest, when the person who had laboured to produce the crop would have reaped it as a reward. In principle this is not implausible but it is not attested elsewhere.

Secondly, it is not clear why Naomi's nearer kinsman goes

back on his initial decision to redeem Naomi's field himself. In order to consider this it is necessary to look carefully at the wording of the verse in which Boaz makes the remark that causes the kinsman to change his mind (4.5). Boaz says 'On the day you acquire the field from the hand of Naomi, Ruth the Moabite widow of the dead man you (also) acquire [reading the *Qere* marginal note 'you acquire' instead of 'I acquire' in the main text] in order to raise up the name of the dead man on his inheritance'. Two interpretative possibilities arise depending on whether the correct wording is taken to be 'you will acquire' or 'I will acquire'. If Boaz is telling the man that if he wishes to have the field he must marry Ruth, then perhaps the man is surprised to learn that it is not Naomi he must marry (a widow presumably beyond child-bearing age), but Ruth—a character of whose existence he had perhaps been unaware, and whose ability to produce children could have led to legal complications in the future. Alternatively, if Boaz's surprise statement is that he himself will marry Ruth (so Beattie, Sasson), then the other kinsman may feel that the land could at best be a temporary investment for him, since if Ruth and Boaz have a child that child will eventually reclaim the land as his own. Difficulties attend both suggestions, owing to their speculative nature, and in particular it is not obvious why an heir born to Boaz and Ruth (4.13-15) should also be accounted an heir to Elimelech and Naomi (4.16-17). This difficulty applies whichever way 4.5 is interpreted, and no final explanation is available.

It is nevertheless possible that insufficient account has been paid to the symbolic character of 4.16-17 in particular. The actions of Naomi's neighbours in naming and establishing the reputation of the child (so Sasson), and attributing him to Naomi (v. 17), and the actions of Naomi herself who 'laid him in her bosom, and became his nurse' (v. 16), may contain faint overtones of the presence of birth deities believed to attend the birth of royal babies in Sumerian culture, for example. The functions of these female deities were to establish the fate and hence the future of a newborn male, who, if human, would almost invariably be a future king. Naomi's action likewise seems to reflect instances known from ancient Near Eastern literature in which a royal child is placed on the lap of a deity and is suckled by her. The dual paternity ascribed to Obed could even reflect the manner in which Near Eastern kings sometimes attributed their own birth to divine as well as to human parents. The Hebrews were no doubt more cautious in their estimation of 'divinized kingship' and if it is correct that vestiges of these ancient motifs are present in the unique package of Ruth 4.16-17 then the motifs have been de-mythologized. But they could reinforce the tendency in 4.11-12 to confer divine legitimation on the house of David.

It is a moot point whether the book of Ruth really gives any solid information on legal practice in pre-exilic Israel, or whether the provisions it sketches are either misunderstood or used simply as narrative devices.

For Further Reading

A.A. Anderson, 'The Marriage of Ruth', *JJS* 23 (1978), pp. 171-83.

D.R.G. Beattie, 'The Book of Ruth as Evidence for Israelite Legal Practice', *VT* 24 (1974), pp. 251-67.

E.W. Davies, 'Ruth IV 5 and the duties of the *goʾel*', *VT* 33 (1983), pp. 231-34.

R. Gordis, 'Love, Marriage and Business in the Book of Ruth: A Chapter in Hebrew Customary Law', in H.N. Bream (ed.), *A Light Unto My Path, Fs. JM Myers* (Gettysburg Theological Studies IV; Gettysburg: Temple University Press, 1974), pp. 241-64.

D.A. Leggett, *The Levirate and Go'el Institutions in the Old Testament with Special Attention to the Book of Ruth* (Cherry Hill, NJ: Mack, 1974).

B.A. Levine, 'In Praise of the Israelite *Mispaha*: Legal Themes in the Book of Ruth', in H.B. Huffmon *et al.* (eds.), *The Quest for the Kingdom of God: Studies in Honor of G.E. Mendenhall* (Winona Lake, IN: Eisenbrauns, 1983), pp. 95-106.

T. Thompson and D. Thompson, 'Some Legal Problems in the Book of Ruth', *VT* 18 (1968), pp. 79-99.

Also useful are:

C.M. Carmichael, 'A Ceremonial Crux: Removing a Man's Sandal as a Female Gesture of Contempt', *JBL* 96 (1977), pp. 321-36.

Kirsten Nielsen, 'Le choix contre le droit dans le livre de Ruth. De l'aire de battage au tribunal', *VT* 35 (1985), pp. 201-12.

S.B. Parker, 'The Marriage Blessing in Israelite and Ugaritic Literature', *JBL* 95 (1976), pp. 23-30.

There is a sequence of articles in JSOT 5 (1978) on these matters:
D.R.G. Beattie, 'Ruth III', pp. 39-48.
—'Redemption in Ruth and Related Matters: A Response to JM Sasson', pp. 65-68.
J.M. Sasson, 'Ruth III: a Response', pp. 49-51.
—'The Issue of ge'ullah in Ruth', pp. 52-64.

4

RUTH
TEXT AND CANON

The Text and Versions

IN TOTAL CONTRAST to the book of Esther, the book of Ruth raises no great text-critical problems. Scholars as varied as Sasson, Rudolph and Hubbard all regard the Hebrew text as sound (although Joüon has reservations). It is not possible to reconstruct a series of stages in the development of Ruth from a study of the ancient versions.

Thus although fragments of a few Hebrew manuscripts of Ruth have been found at Qumran they closely resemble the Hebrew text we already know (the Masoretic text). Of the Qumran finds, 2QRuth*a* contains fragments of text from 2.13 to 4.4 probably dating from the first century of the Christian era; 2QRuth*b* contains pieces of 3.13-18; and 4QRuth*a* contains fourteen lines of ch. 1. The ancient Jewish translation of Ruth from Hebrew into the vernacular Aramaic (known as the Targum), is such a close paraphrase of the Hebrew that Sasson finds it of little help in his philological investigations; and the ancient Syriac translation, though much more free, is of disputed value for comparative purposes as its date and provenance are uncertain. The Greek Septuagint translations, though showing some fluidity as between one manuscript and another (and there are fifty of them), are rarely such as to improve our understanding of individual passages of Ruth.

However, it should be mentioned that the Septuagint of Ruth was used by Rahlfs in 1922 as a pilot project for the classification of the Greek manuscripts generally into families, a project which was intended to be extended to the whole of the Old Testament, but was never completed. It is thus on the basis of texts of Ruth that the families of manuscripts known as Hexaplaric, proto-Lucianic, *kaige*, and Old Greek were first established. Thus the study of Ruth has inadvertently illuminated the possible history of translation of the biblical texts generally. Cross (whose work has not, however, been universally accepted), tried to build on the work of Rahlfs by matching the main families of Greek manuscripts to postulated corresponding families within the underlying Hebrew tradition. These separate strands of Hebrew tradition were supposed to have evolved through the geographical separation of the main Jewish communities from the time of the exile onward. The Hebrew tradition underlying the Old Greek was supposed to stem from Egypt; the Hebrew Palestinian tradition gave rise to the proto-Lucianic family of Greek texts; and the Babylonian Hebrew tradition gave rise to the *kaige* family.

The Masoretic text of Ruth has some peculiarities which should be mentioned. There is a fairly high incidence of marginal notes (Qere) which correct errors in the sacred text (1.8; 2.1; 3.3, 4, 14; 4.4, 5); several examples of marginal insertions (2.11; 3.5, 17); and one example of a deletion indicated in the margin (3.12). None, however, is of great significance from the viewpoint of the interpreter (Sasson, and others).

A second feature of the Hebrew of Ruth is apparent gender confusion: masculine verbs or suffixes are found with feminine antecedents. Research so far has chiefly sought an explanation for the suffixes, but none has won the day, for example, the mismatch has been described either as a feature of late Hebrew; or as a dialectical variant (which could be early); or as a dual construction (appropriate in describing pairs of objects); or perhaps just as colloquial. No one knows.

There are, in compensation, very few places at which the text resists translation without emendation. The most difficult words to render into English come at the end of 2.7, and can be translated literally as 'this [masc.] her sitting/dwelling the house (a) little' (nrsv says 'without resting even for a moment'). Thus the Hebrew is unclear, and unfortunately the versions diverge and cannot resolve the matter. A full discussion of the problems posed by this verse as a whole is provided by Campbell (pp. 94-96) who in fact leaves all but the first few words untranslated. Although the verse comes at an important turning point in the book, as it immediately precedes the account of the first meeting between Ruth and Boaz, it is unlikely that anything turns on it. A more important crux for interpretation is 4.5, which has been discussed above in relation to the legal background of the book.

Canonicity

A further contrast between Ruth and Esther is that there was no difficulty over the acceptance of Ruth into the canon. It is true that talmudic tradition (*Meg.* 7a) says that 'Ruth, the Song of Songs and Esther make the hands unclean'—meaning that they make the dangerous contagion of holiness cling to the hands of one who touches the scroll, and this statement hints that some held an opinion to the contrary which is well attested for Esther but not otherwise known of Ruth. But the statement does not necessarily mean that there was a problem over Ruth's acceptance into the canon. The divine name is often mentioned in it (YHWH eighteen times, Shaddai twice and *ʾelōhīm* four times), its style and content are above reproach, and it has an important connection with the traditions concerning David. On the other hand, it is possible that the rabbis found it problematic in respect of its conflicts with the Pentateuchal laws. Rabbinic tradition resolves the problem of the book's conflict with Deut. 23.3-6 (forbidding mixed marriages such as those of Mahlon, Chilion and Boaz) by explaining that the law permits Israelite men to marry out, but not Israelite women.

The location of Ruth in the canon presents more of a problem, since, as already noted, it appears both in the Writings (in Jewish tradition) and in the Prophets (in the Septuagint tradition). The question arises as to whether the Septuagint continues a tradition that was originally Jewish (Gerleman) or whether the placing of Ruth in the Hebrew canon should be regarded as the original (Rudolph).

The placing attested in the Hebrew Bible is supported by

the Babylonian Talmud (*b. Bat* 14b) and *4 Ezra* 14.44-46 (the latter c. 100 BC), which affirm the existence of a twenty-four book canon with Ruth among the Writings. The principle of arrangement is chronological, and Ruth is placed first among the Writings. The alternative tradition is attested by church Fathers such as Origen, Jerome and Melito (all of them scholars who took trouble to investigate the Hebrew tradition), and by an ambiguous remark in Josephus (*Apion* 1.8, 38-42) to the effect that there are twenty-two books in the Hebrew bible, a number that only coincides with the actual twenty four known to us if two books are merged with others: the implication is that Ruth is counted with Judges, and Lamentations with Jeremiah, though this does not exhaust the theoretical possibilities. Most scholars would agree that this line of evidence is the weaker of the two (so Hubbard, for example, despite his belief that Ruth could be pre-exilic), since it is difficult to push back the origins of this tradition beyond the evidence given above. On the face of it, Ruth is more likely to have belonged originally to the Writings and been 'promoted' to the Prophets than *vice versa*.

An interesting postscript to this point is that a number of literary links have been noted between the ending of Judges (chs. 19–21, the story of the Levite's concubine) and Ruth. It is probable that the Judges material is a late addition to the book, but still the range of comparisons is striking: in addition to a number of grammatical correspondences such as the shared use of the idiom 'to take wives' (using the unusual verb *nāśʾa*; Ruth 1.4 and Judg. 21.23), both stories have a connection with Bethlehem in Judah, although the events in the one are inverse to those in the other. In each case sojourners require hospitality, which in Ruth is given and in Judges is first offered but then abused, and the events which unfold in Ruth, leading to the continuation of a familial line which proves to be that of David, are in direct contrast to those which transpire in Judges, with the whole tribe of Benjamin in danger of extinction as a result of the breakdown of law. The comparison—or rather contrast—could have invited the 'promotion' of Ruth to the Prophets.

Within the context of the Writings, the placing of Ruth also varies. Despite the Talmudic tradition that it is the first of the Writings, it is in practice usually found in modern Hebrew Bibles (based on the excellent Leningrad manuscript dated to 1008 or 1009 AD) after Proverbs, which ends with a poem in praise of a worthy woman, *ʾēšeth-ḥayil*, such as Ruth surely is meant to be.

Ruth among the Megilloth

It remains to discuss the inclusion of Ruth among the five Megilloth, or little scrolls appointed to be read at festivals. The organizing of the five into a group probably dates back only to the sixth–ninth centuries AD, and within it Ruth may be found either first (in traditionally chronological order of authorship, since it was allegedly written by Samuel), or second in the order of the festival sequence, celebrating the Feast of Weeks or Shabuʾot.

It is not completely certain why Ruth should be the lection for this feast, also called Pentecost (alluding to its date fifty days after the first day of Passover). It is not a festival aetiology, as Esther is, nor is Pentecost specifically referred to within it. But the connection is invited by the fact that Ruth is set in the period between Passover and the barley harvest on the one hand (1.22), and Pentecost and the wheat harvest on the other hand (2.23). Furthermore, Ruth's acceptance of the Israelite way of life, often referred to as her 'conversion', make her story very suitable for a festival which is not only agricultural but has also (in typical Israelite fashion) been given a secondary historical significance as commemorating the giving of the Law on Mount Sinai. Nor is that all, for traditionally David is supposed to have been born and to have died at this season of the year.

For Further Reading

In addition to relevant material in the commentaries, see:

D.R.G. Beattie, 'Ruth 2.7 and Midrash', ZAW 99 (1987), pp. 422-23, a different view to that of:

Avi Hurvitz, 'Ruth 2.7—A Midrashic Gloss?', *ZAW* 95 (1983), pp. 121-23.

R. Thornhill, 'The Greek Text of the Book of Ruth: A Grouping of Manuscripts According to Origen's Hexapla', *VT* 3 (1953), pp. 239-49.

On the connection between Ruth and Judges 19-21 see:

R.G. Boling, *Judges* (AB; Garden City, NY: Doubleday, 1975).

5

RUTH
LITERARY QUESTIONS

MODERN LITERARY ANALYSIS of the book of Ruth begins with the work of Gunkel, both with his definition of the genre as that of 'novella', and with his breakdown of the contents of the book into eleven major scenes. We have already considered the genre of Ruth both as it compares with that of Esther and as it bears upon the vexed question of the date of the book by allowing comparisons to be drawn with other biblical books or stories within books whose date is thought to be more secure on other grounds. But it remains to consider the genre of Ruth as a topic in its own right, able to determine what questions may properly be asked of the text (so that if, for example, the story is folkloristic, it should not be used as if it could answer questions of law, and so on).

The category of novella as described by Gunkel is rather broad. Essentially it is more concerned to describe situations and characters than to report facts; it will make good use of dialogues; it will be brief but with a number of episodes; it will be well crafted; and it will be fictional. Within the whole spectrum of literary activity, which Jolles believed to be reducible to nine 'simple forms' (*Einfache Formen*, 1930) namely the legend, saga, myth, riddle, proverb, case, memoir, tale and joke/pun, the novella is equivalent to the 'tale' (Sasson).

In order to narrow the category, Gunkel suggested that Ruth was also close to the 'idyll', a simple pastoral story with no evil characters in it. But other approaches are possible, and to those such as Campbell who feel that 'novella' is suggestive of insufficiently serious intention and exclusive of any possible historicity, the term 'short story' is preferred. The short story Campbell defined as semi-poetic in literary quality (especially in the characters' speeches); interested in typical or ordinary people (even if they and their actions ultimately prove to be of wider import); instructive as well as entertaining (specifically, in the case of Ruth, showing God's purpose at work); and of high quality in its wedding of literary artistry with depth of purpose.

Campbell in fact believes that the short story was a new literary form which appeared in Israel without need of foreign borrowings, and indeed that if its origins are early in the monarchical period then very little precedent can be found for it, of any kind. He appeals to the authenticity of its portrayal of village life to reinforce his hypothesis, though without claiming that Ruth is primarily a historical work.

In similar vein, the structure of Ruth can be rooted in covenant history by setting it in a sequence with the stories of Lot in Genesis 13 and 19 and of Judah and Tamar in Genesis 38. Each arguably follows the same structure in which the sequence of actions comprises: (1) descent and separation; (2) disaster resulting from separation; (3) abandonment, with the only hope of the preservation of the family residing in a woman; (4) redemption, as a nearer kinsman is made to accept responsibility for continuation of the family; (5) a bed trick, in which the woman takes the initiative; (6) a celebration; (7) a levirate union; and (8) the issue.

This, however, has not been the last word on the subject by any means, as Ruth has also been more closely defined as a 'comedy' by Phyllis Trible; as a historical novel by Robertson; as a 'subversive parable' by Lacocque; and as a folktale, or at least as 'folkloristic' (i.e. written on a folktale model, but not necessarily told originally as an oral folktale), by Sasson. This last alternative represents a radical departure from Campbell's view, since for him it is precisely the 'fairy-tale' elements in the obviously late stories (such as Esther) which show that they are late, as such features are in his view a non-original and degenerate feature of the short story genre.

Ruth as Folkloristic

The fullest attempt to measure Ruth against a folkloristic standard is that of Sasson, who approaches the task by taking as his standard the work of Vladimir Propp (1928) on the morphology of Russian fairy stories. Propp was chiefly interested in those elements of plot which propel a narrative from one action to another. These he called 'functions', concluding on the basis of an analysis of a great number of tales that these functions were limited in number (he counted thirty-one in all) and that although not all need be included in any particular story they would always appear in the same sequence. The functions would be carried out by up to seven *dramatis personae* who would be interesting not for the portrayal of their character in any individual sense, but for their function in furthering the plot in the necessary manner. As with the functions, so with the *dramatis personae*, not all of whom need be included in every story: Ruth, for example, lacks a 'villain', but it does have a 'despatcher' (Naomi), a 'hero' (Ruth), a 'sought-for person' (Obed) and a 'false hero' (the unnamed man in 4.1ff.). The function of Boaz is complex and twofold: he appears first as a 'donor/helper', and secondly as a 'hero' himself.

The story unfolds according to the Proppian sequence. To simplify somewhat, chs. 1 and 2 (Move I) contain preparatory material sketching the scene and setting up a lack or absence, in this case the poverty and vulnerability of the women (1.1-6), which it is the role of the hero to remedy. Ruth is identified as the hero (1.7-17) who will depart on a quest to make good what is lacking (1.18–2.2). Next the donor is introduced (Boaz) who will help the heroine in her task but may interrogate and test her too, until a preliminary resolution is reached (2.3-22). A new series of events functionally parallel to the first is described in 3.1-13 (Move II). At this point Sasson believes that a transfer of role occurs, as Boaz himself becomes the hero (3.14-15) (in this connection it is interesting that the last words of 3.15 'then he went into the city' have long puzzled commentators who thought that Ruth should be the subject of this verb; Sasson finds evidence here to support his claim that it is now Boaz who is the questing hero). Finally, after some 'connective' material in 3.16-18 (i.e. material which Sasson cannot classify in relation to a Proppian function) the tale proceeds in a new direction (Move III), with Boaz arriving at the city gate as an unrecognized hero, who must challenge the false hero (4.1ff.). As he does this successfully, the task and the quest of the story are fulfilled and the hero receives his reward (4.15). The remainder (Move IV) in 4.16-22 has the character of the beginning of a new tale. The result is a completely satisfying tale in which no expectations are left unfulfilled, for 'the protagonists fully carry out assignments that were perfected generations before Ruth'.

Some stresses and strains are evident in the attempt to match Ruth to this formalist schema, and Sasson himself has always said that the Proppian categories need to be 'refined and perhaps redefined' in order to become more applicable to biblical and other ancient Near Eastern texts. He would also add the proviso that Ruth, though folkloristic in form, should not be referred to as a folktale since that implies a long period of oral transmission which cannot be demonstrated to have occurred. In the second edition of his work, Sasson also expresses some regret that the Proppian aspects of his analysis—actually confined to part of a chapter at the end of his philological commentary (pp. 196-218)—have received what he regards as a disproportionate amount of attention. It is, however, natural that this very distinctive piece of work which has implications for the study of folkloristic elements in biblical literature generally should have generated so much interest.

Ruth's Antecedents

Although it has been argued (Campbell 1975) that the Hebrew short story was a new literary form of which Ruth is one of the first exemplars, and that the search for earlier literary and thematic 'stages' is a blind alley since (even if such stages existed) we cannot know of them, a number of attempts have been made to identify such earlier stages.

Again we return to Gunkel, who argued that the main motif of the story was that of the loyal, childless widow who obtains an heir for her deceased husband, a motif going back to Egyptian fairy tales and also reminiscent of the Isis and Osiris myth (in which the god Horus is conceived by Isis from the dead Osiris). In Israel, the elements of magic and sorcery would have been unacceptable from the earliest times, however, and this element of the tale was replaced by recourse to human legal mechanisms such as levirate marriage, and first appeared in its new guise in the story of Judah and Tamar in Genesis 38. Only secondarily did it appear in the Naomi story (to which Ruth herself was added later) becoming progressively less coarse and more refined. This hypothesis has won little acceptance not only because it is obviously speculative but also because it is 'atomistic', dealing with isolated segments of narrative while tending to ignore the theme and motivation of the story as a whole (Sasson).

Criticism can also be made of the theory that Ruth was originally part of Canaanite oral poetry (perhaps an ancient nursery tale), which was written down either after the exile (Myers), or in several stages commencing in the ninth to eighth centuries with the addition of the concept of *ḥesed* (lovingkindess), and completed after the exile with the addition of the genealogical material and the note on the defunct shoe custom in 4.7 (Glanzman). First, efforts to show that Ruth is fundamentally pure poetry (Myers) must be judged to have failed, partly because scholars are still divided over the identification of the principles on which Hebrew poetry worked (neither stress counts nor syllable counts give satisfactory results in material normally classified as poetry, like the Psalms), and partly because it has emerged from Myers's work that if the whole of Ruth is to be classified as poetry it is necessary to use more than one type of diagnostic principle—changing them over in a manner that looks arbitrary—and indeed to make strategic emendations to the MT before the counting process (whether of syllables or stresses) begins. Secondly, the commonly made assumption that poetry is necessarily more ancient than prose does not bear investigation: there is no obvious reason why a poem should have been transferred into prose, and prose arguably seems a more suitable vehicle for this rather domestic story than early poetry (Campbell).

A third theory or family of theories about the background

of Ruth abandons the quest for its original literary form and concentrates on its possible function as a fertility cult legend. Although comparisons have been drawn with legends from Mesopotamia, Greece and Canaan, the Mesopotamian and Greek options are now 'practically extinct' (Sasson) having been heavily criticized by Rowley (1965); any parallels with the course of events in the Eleusian myths are due to the fact that both independently fit the folktale pattern. Barbara Gail Green in an unpublished dissertation dealing with field and seed symbolism in Ruth has found some twenty motifs which the book shares with a variety of stories from other cultures, including the Iroquois. The Canaanite version of the theory is, however, enjoying reconsideration, owing to the fact that motifs connected with fertility do cluster thickly in Ruth, and the threshing floor where an important part of the action takes place is a site which always has cultic overtones in the ancient world. In addition, the name 'Bethlehem' meaning 'house of bread' (or more strongly 'House of [the god] Lehem') could refer to a cultic centre. More boldly still, Moab as the home of the chthonic deity Chemosh can be understood as a symbol of the Netherworld from which Ruth emerges to partake of the life of Yahweh's 'house of bread'. It is argued that in the original legend, the famine at the outset of the story would have been the result, not the cause, of Naomi's departure, and renewed fertility in Judah the result of her return (see Wright; Sheehan). This too, however, is highly speculative.

Fourthly, a more modest and correspondingly more successful proposal has been made to the effect that Ruth represents the combination of two pre-existing Israelite oral tales, one concerning Naomi (Variant A) and the other Ruth (Variant B), both stemming from Bethlehem and the clan of Perez, and sharing the common theme of 'reversal of feminine fortune'. The best evidence in favour of this duality is that the present book seems undecided over who the heroine is (and indeed who is redeemed and who becomes a mother with the birth of Obed!), Naomi or Ruth. Brenner would then set the story in a sequence with the tales of Lot's daughters (Gen. 19.30-38) and of Judah and Tamar (Gen. 38) as traditional material explaining both David's connections with foreigners, and his weakness for women, as being in his blood. However, on the face of it there is no compelling reason why Variants A and B should have been combined to serve such a purpose, and more importantly the book as it stands does appear to be an authorial unity (with the possible exception of 4.17, 18-22), and this is one of the points on which scholars are virtually unanimous.

It only remains to question the assumption that Ruth necessarily began as an oral tale at all. Even though this might at first sight look entirely uncontroversial and rather plausible (see for example Campbell's discussion of the role of the 'singer of tales' in ancient Israel), it can be objected that the book lacks the requisite percentage of formulaic language and even an insufficiently formalized story pattern. Even Sasson would agree that despite its folkloristic qualities it is more likely a written story modelled on a folktale pattern.

The Structure of Ruth

The structure of Ruth as set out by Gunkel and followed by many other scholars (e.g. by Murphy in the *Forms of the Old Testament Literature* series), is as follows: 1.1-5 setting the scene; 1.6-18 Naomi returns home; 1.19-22 interlude, arrival of Naomi and Ruth in Bethlehem; 2.1-17, Ruth the Moabitess finds favour in the field of Boaz; 2.18-23, interlude, Ruth reports to Naomi; 3.1-5, Naomi's plan; 3.6-15, Boaz pledges himself to Ruth at the threshing floor; 3.16-18, interlude, Ruth reports to Naomi; 4.1-12, the transaction at the Bethlehem gate; 4.13-17, conclusion, the birth of a son; 4.18-22, genealogical appendix. These scenes are defined by changes in the location and sometimes in the direction of the action, and are often given cohesion internally and with one another by catchwords and reiteration, such as *šûb* 'return' (twelve times throughout ch. 1).

More simply, the work may be divided into four 'episodes' (so Hubbard, for example), each corresponding to a chapter (none of Gunkel's scenes bridges a chapter division), and perhaps excluding the genealogies in 4.17, 18-22 as secondary. In favour of this general scheme is the fact that each chapter can be seen as 'centred' upon a particular verse or verses

(vv. 11-13 for ch. 1; v. 10 for ch. 2; v. 9 for ch. 3, and v. 11 for ch. 4), with the rest of the material in the episode being symmetrically arranged around the centre. A special study of chiastic structures in ch. 1 has been carried out by Hallaire. In similar vein, a larger symmetry is sometimes identified between chs. 2 and 3 in particular (so Bertman; this is of the course the section of the book in which according to Sasson's very different structural analysis Move II replicates the greater part of Move I). The hypothesis that the story is symmetrically arranged is less successful in regard to chs. 1 and 4.

Literary Quality and Paronomasia

If Ruth cannot actually be put in the category of poetry there is nevertheless wide agreement that it is prose of a very high quality which frequently borders on poetry, containing many examples of parallelism and of vocabulary and idioms with a poetic flavour, such that it has been called 'lyrical' (Gunkel), or 'ceremonial-literary' (Campbell). It is also worth noting that of all the books of the Old Testament it has the highest ratio of dialogue to narrative text, some fifty-five verses out of eighty-five (Joüon), which is suggestive of its dramatic potential. A number of other features of the book which make it well suited for public recitation or performance are given by Sasson (pp. 226-27).

A feature of Old Testament narrative which is amply demonstrated in Ruth is that because there are so few digressions there is little opportunity for the audience or the reader to relax, so that the narrative is constantly suspenseful. It is also (in Auerbach's immortal phrase) 'fraught with background'. The meaning of this expression may be understood by considering how needless details are stripped away in the story-telling, so that the hearer or reader hears dialogue and sees actions and has to deduce the motivation of the character for himself or herself (just as happens in real life). This means that the audience has to contribute heavily to the understanding of character in the story (again, as in real life), and although it is typical of all ancient story-telling that only two characters are ever engaged in conversation at one time, the audience is drawn into supposing how the unseen, unheard presence of the characters who are presently in the 'background' (including God himself) is in fact affecting the choices made by the characters who are on view. This is a topic that will recur in relation to the theology of Ruth, which arguably features the theme of the hiddenness of providence.

A brief classification of the great range of techniques used may be found in Sasson (pp. 223-25), but the flavour can perhaps be appreciated by selecting a few examples (inevitably a matter of personal preference). The author seems very fond of playing with hidden numbers, especially sevens, threes, and multiples thereof. Thus the name of Naomi is repeated twenty-one times (three times seven); Bethlehem, Moab and 'Moabitess' occur seven times; Judah three times; and in Boaz's oath 'as the Lord lives' (*ḥay* YHWH, 3.13) the numerical value of the Hebrew characters in 'lives' namely *ḥeth* (eight) and *yōd* (ten) total eighteen, which is the number of times the name Yhwh occurs in the whole book. Other examples of this nature could be listed.

The book is also characterized by the presence of patterning which does not depend on numerology, such as the deployment of sets of opposites: famine/plenty, barreness/fruitfulness, old age/youth, isolation/community and reward/punishment (Rauber), to which Trible has added male/female, death/life and tradition/innovation. These may be 'bracketing devices' forcing the audience to focus on the material which the narrator thinks important, and should not be confused with the technique of *inclusio* whereby a phrase recurs at the beginning and end of a unit of material so as to 'frame' the contents (though examples of *inclusio* are also found in Ruth).

On a still smaller level, chiasms have been noted in which a pair of words is used twice, with the order reversed on the second occurrence (Campbell): husband/boys (1.3 and 5); go/return (1.8 and 12); Shaddai/Yahweh (1.20 and 21); lament/kiss (1.9 and 14); elders/people (4.9 and 11); and Mahlon and Chilion (1.2, 5 and 4.9).

Further features include great use of assonance (2.10 is often cited) and punning. Campbell says 'one of his [the author's] techniques is to establish a particular Hebrew vocable as a key word in a particular scene and to repeat it frequently throughout the scene, often picking it up in another scene to serve as a linking device'; an associated technique is to 'plumb the assorted nuances of a particular vocable'.

The author seems deliberately to use key words and phrases twice, for example, 'security' (1.9; 3.1); 'empty' (1.21; 3.17); 'substance/worthy' (2.1; 3.11 [cf. 4.11]); take note/ regard (2.10; 2.19); 'wing(s)' (2.12; 3.19); although some are used three or four times, such as *ḥesed* (1.8; 2.20; 3.10) and 'cling/attach/stay close' (1.14; 2.8, 21, 23). In each case the first use of the word foreshadows what is to come, as problems are first stated and later resolved.

Characteristically names—which have meanings—are used to suggest the mood of the story. Thus the name of Elimelech 'my God is king' is suggestive of the future of his line, which will issue in the birth of David, the king who is God's vice-regent on earth. Naomi 'my gracious/pleasant one' asks to be called Mara 'bitter one' as her troubles press home (1.20); her dead sons are Mahlon 'sick' and Chilion 'weakening/pining', while her daughters-in-law are Orphah 'cloud/drip/nape' (back of neck = turned her back, or cloud = not abundant in water?), and Ruth herself whose name may mean 'friend' (or 'saturated' = abundant in water). Boaz's name appropriately means 'strength (is) in him' or 'he comes in strength', and his son Obed 'servant' is the ancestor of the Davidic kings who were servants of the Lord. Enough has perhaps been said to show that Ruth has been carefully wrought, down to the last detail.

Status of 4.17, 18-22

In the light of the above we return to the question of the originality of the genealogical material, which has often been regarded as suspect. So far as 4.17 is concerned the most complete consideration to date is probably that of Hubbard (1988), who does not regard the verse as original. It is strange that 'the women' name Ruth's child—and do it twice (v. 17a and 17b)—and that the name of Obed does not appear in the women's first proclamation. One popular explanation has been that the word *šēm* ('name') has replaced the original name (perhaps Ben-noam) in v. 17a (so Eissfeldt, in his *Introduction to the Old Testament*), while v. 17b is secondary.

An alternative view is that v. 17b is original because 17a would not really be complete without it: v. 17a is not in itself a name-giving formula but has some separate purpose such as formally announcing the birth of a son to his father (or, here, to Naomi) (compare Jer. 20.14-18). The giving of the name in 17b is thus required to complete the scene.

Fewer scholars feel able to defend the originality of the genealogy in 4.18-22, largely on the ground that genealogy is form-critically quite distinct from story forms, at least in the modern mind. It has clear connections with a more detailed genealogy in 1 Chron. 2.5-15, and keys onto the mention of Perez the ancestor of Boaz in 4.12, ignoring the emphasis of the narrator who thinks of Obed as Naomi's son and Elimelech's heir, and strengthens the connection of David to the story. Even so, work on the nature of ancient genealogy-writing done in the 60s and 70s has shown how purposive and creative an art it was, opening the way to the possibility that it was, after all, always part of the story (Sasson; Gordis 1974), or at least that it is in harmony with the rest of the book theologically (Loretz 1960). Its tenfold numbering mirrors the ten years of 1.4 and the ten elders of 4.2; it balances 1.1-5, the account of the near-extinction of Elimelech's line, with assurance of the continuity of that line; and generally underlines the great themes of the story: Ruth's great reward for her loyalty, and the faithfulness of God's providence through the generations.

An alternative view is that of McCarthy and Riley, who suggest that both v. 17b and 4.18-22 are additions attracted to the original story by the Bethlehem connection (cf. David in 1 Sam. 16.1); contacts with Moab (1 Sam. 22.3-4 states that David's parents lived there at one time); and mention of Perez in 4.12 recalling another levirate marriage in the Davidic line. The result was that the story of Ruth was absorbed into the traditions concerning David.

For Further Reading

On Ruth's Antecedents:

A. Brenner, 'Naomi and Ruth', *VT* 33 (1983), pp. 385-97.

C. Fontaine, 'The Deceptive Goddess', *Semeia* 42 (1988), pp. 84-102.

J.M. Mayes, *The Linguistic and Literary Form of the Book of Ruth* (Leiden: Brill, 1955).

J.F.K. Sheehan, 'The Word of God as Myth: the Book of Ruth', in R.J. Clifford (ed.), *The Word in the World. Essays in Honor of F.L. Moriarty, SJ* (Cambridge: Weston College Press, 1973), pp. 35-46.

G.R.H. Wright, 'The Mother-Maid at Bethlehem', *ZAW* 98 (1986), pp. 56-72.

On The Structure of Ruth:

In addition to Gow, *The Book of Ruth* see:

S. Bertman, 'Symmetrical Design in the Book of Ruth', *JBL* 84 (1965), pp. 165-68.

J. Hallaire, 'Un jeu de structures dans le livre de Ruth', *Nouvelle Revue Théologique* 113 (1991), pp. 708-27.

E.R. Wendland, 'Structural Symmetry and Its Significance in the Book of Ruth', in P.C. Stine (ed.), *Issues in Bible Translation* (UBS Monograph, 3; New York: United Bible Societies, 1983), pp. 30-63.

On Literary Quality and Paronomasia:

Adele Berlin, 'Poetics in the Book of Ruth', in *Poetics and the Interpretation of Biblical Narrative* (Sheffield: Almond Press, 1983).

M. Bernstein, 'Two Multivalent Readings in the Ruth Narrative', *JSOT* 50 (1991), pp. 15-26.

Calum M. Carmichael, ' "Treading" in the Book of Ruth', *ZAW* 92 (1980), pp. 248-66.

D.N. Fewell and D.M. Gunn, *Compromising Redemption: Relating Characters in the Book of Ruth* (Literary Currents in Biblical Interpretation; Louisville, Westminster/John Knox, 1990).

—' "A son is born to Naomi": Literary Allusions and Interpretation in the Book of Ruth', *JSOT* 40 (1988), pp. 99-108 (see also P.W. Coxon, 'Was Naomi a Scold? A Response to Fewell and Gunn', *JSOT* 45 [1989], pp. 25-37).

—'Is Coxon a Scold? On Responding to the Book of Ruth', *JSOT* 45 (1989), pp. 39-43.

—'Boaz, Pillar of Society: Measures of Worth in the Book of Ruth', *JSOT* 45 (1989), pp. 45-59.

R. Gordis, 'Personal Names in Ruth—A Note on Biblical Etymologies', *Judaism* 139 (1986), pp. 298-300.

D.F. Rauber, 'Literary Values in the Bible: The Book of Ruth', *JBL* 89 (1970), pp. 27-37.

P. Trible, 'A Human Comedy: The Book of Ruth', in *Literary Interpretations of Biblical Narratives* (ed. K.R.R. Gros Louis with J.S. Ackerman; Nashville: Abingdon Press, 1982), II, pp. 161-90.

Further items will be found listed in D.F. Watson and A.J. Hauser (eds.), *Rhetorical Criticism of the Bible* (Leiden: Brill, 1994), pp. 53-54.

On the Status of 4.17, 18-22:

R.L. Hubbard, 'Ruth IV 7. A New Solution', *VT* 38 (1988), pp. 293-301.

O. Loretz, 'Das Verhältnis zwischen Rut-Story und David-Genealogie im Rut-Buch', *ZAW* 89 (1977), pp. 124-26.

6

RUTH
THEOLOGY AND PURPOSE

The Themes and Theology of Ruth

IN ORDER TO CONSIDER the theology and purpose of Ruth, it is worth first trying to isolate the main themes of the book. There are at least two. First there is the theme of the rescue of Elimelech's line. Yahweh brings this about (4.14), causing Naomi to return to her own country (1.6, 22) so that her emptiness can be turned into fullness, and her childlessness to the birth of an heir for Elimelech. Even Ruth is said to 'return', notwithstanding that she is a foreigner (1.7, 22; 2.6), as if she represents the reintegration of one of the lines issuing from Lot back into Israel. Thus the complaints of Naomi at the beginning of the book (1.20-21) are changed into rejoicing at its end. This theme of reversal was remarked upon by Josephus (Ant. 5.9.4) who said that the book of Ruth showed how God wonderfully lifts up the lowly and brings down the proud. A related but distinct issue is that it tells the story of the provenance of David, which would in any case be a matter of great interest to Israelite tradition. The fact that David's ancestry was exceptional is underlined by the fact of the initial hopelessness of the situation, as the bereaved women face famine in Moab.

The other major theme is that of *ḥesed* (1.8; 2.20; 3.10) sometimes translated as 'lovingkindness' and also implying steadfastness and loyalty. From its first mention by Naomi (1.8), wishing that God's *ḥesed* may be shown to Ruth and Orpah, the story's characters consistently pray for rewards for those who show *ḥesed* to one another (2.11-12, 20; 3.10)—and see those prayers answered. It is true that *ḥesed* is not specifically mentioned in the women's praise of Yahweh for all his blessings in 4.14, but the birth of Obed is the culmination of all the rewards for which they have been wishing and working.

Putting these major themes together, it can be seen that God uses the faithfulness of ordinary people to achieve great things. And this is arguably an important feature of the book's theology. Quite how the nature of the relationship between divine and human endeavour is to be interpreted is, however, controversial. The following statement is based chiefly on the work of Hubbard, and outlines the problem.

No one would deny that the people and actions portrayed in Ruth are actually rather ordinary; there are no miracles or wonders, and although Yahweh is often mentioned he seems not to intervene directly. It is therefore open to question whether the author intends the reader to see the story as a parade example of divine providence, or alternatively of human initiative. Hubbard begins his argument from the assertion that the author wishes to portray 'Yahweh, God of Israel' (2.12) as the God of the covenant, who will 'show *ḥesed* to thousands of them that love me and keep my commandments' (Deut. 5.10//Exod. 20.6); that is, as the God who gives both famine and plenty (1.6) as he did in the wilderness, and who cares for the poor and vulnerable (1.16; 2.12). He is a God who, from the first moment of his promise to Abraham that in him all the families of the earth would be blessed (Gen. 12.3), has let it be known that he is God of all peoples. The Priestly name El-Shaddai used of him by Naomi in 1.20-21 recalls these ancient promises. Paradoxically, the very fact that Naomi complains of the treatment Shaddai has meted out to her suggests that she does regard him as the divine ruler who is ultimately responsible for the right ordering of the world (compare 1.8; and the straightforward blessing-prayers of 2.12; 3.10). The *ḥesed* which is a characteristic theme of the book is assumed to be a constituent element of the moral order of the universe, which Yahweh oversees.

However, the only two reports of God's direct intervention

occur in 1.6 and 4.13 (both concerning fertility), and although the beginning and the end are the most likely places to look for interpretative keys in a short story, it is not absolutely clear to what extent God is involved in between times. He is invoked seven times in prayers and blessings (1.8-9; 2.12, 19, 20; 3.10; 4.11-12; 4.14), twice in oath formulae (1.17; 3.13), and twice in Naomi's complaints (1.13, 20-21). All the prayers are answered by the end of the story, and presumably only God answers prayer. Thus it is as though he is an invisible character in the story, mediating between Naomi and Boaz (who never meet) even when he is not portrayed as intervening directly. Hals therefore argues that the author must mean to imply that divine action occurs *through human agents*.

This viewpoint is widely accepted, but not universally. Sasson, for example, is more inclined to see the point of the story in the way the characters help themselves. Indeed from the point of view of folklore analysis which understands such stories to proceed along well-worn tracks there is no necessity for divine intervention, other than any which may be supplied to the hero by numinous donors/helpers whom he (or she) meets along the way. Thus when Ruth 2.3 says that Ruth 'happened' to come to Boaz's part of the fields (cf. 2.4; 3.1-13, 18; 4.1 and even 4.17b) it is describing not divine providence but an accident or even a ploy which the human actors will initiate or respond to through their own resources. It is not clear that Ruth has come to seek refuge under the wing (*kānāp*) of the God of Israel as Boaz says (2.12 cf. 3.9), for in fact she chooses a man as her 'redeemer', and it is his *kānāp* that is spread over her in token of his acceptance of the role. Previously, she has chosen to 'stay close' to the young men (2.21) when he has told her to stay close to the young women! Certainly the human characters themselves never recognize God's activity until after the fact.

Sasson, in the second edition of his *Philological Commentary*, expresses some regret at his previous insistence on this point of view, but it remains true to say that the book does not generalize about the workings of any providence there may be—suggesting that behaviour of a certain kind will oblige God always to respond in the same way, for example.

There is nothing automatic about the book's doctrine of reward. On the contrary, there are moments at which the narrator avoids mentioning God, even when (as in the famous 2.3) he arguably invites the thought of providence. God is not even shown influencing or evaluating the characters' behaviour as he does in the Joseph story and elsewhere (e.g. Gen. 39.21).

One reason could be that the author does not want to show God working intermittent miracles and retreating to a remote observation point in the meantime. He wishes to suggest that God's activity is continuous, but largely hidden in human activities. Acts of *ḥesed*, which conform to Yahweh's will, can be seen as Yahweh's acts. Precisely what this means and how it should be expressed is not clear. Alternative formulations speak of the 'correlation' or 'interpenetration' of divine and human acts (Campbell); or of the 'combination' of the two. Perhaps one could say that Yahweh will honour acts of human *ḥesed* as if they were his own. Hubbard (1989) also brings out the fact that the initiative of Yahweh acts on a higher level than that of the human characters, who can only make secondary responses; comparable is the view of Prinsloo, that Yahweh's ultimate blessings extend well beyond the range of the single family involved in the story.

The book certainly does not romanticize this honour. The demands of *ḥesed* are heavy, as can be seen from the contrast between Orpah (who is not criticized for taking an easier option) and Ruth who is ready to follow Naomi even to death (1.17). Hubbard would argue in addition that *ḥesed* has to be exercised within the law, and that this explains the book's interest in the processes of law.

The Purpose of Ruth

It was noted in Chapter 2 above that arguments about the purpose of Ruth have tended to be related to arguments about the date at which it was written. It is unlikely that an ancient story preserved in the way that Ruth has been is intended solely to entertain, but it has also to be borne in mind that a great story, such as Ruth is often held to be, is not limited to the function it had in its original place and time. The lectionary function which Ruth now has is of course not original, nor an exhaustive function, but apart from that the various options can be reviewed as follows:

To Commend Social Duties Like Levirate Marriage?
Notwithstanding the historical interest in this question, it seems to be an unlikely rationale for the book as a whole, since none of the customs portrayed are given sufficient prominence to account for the purpose of the book as a whole, and they are poorly articulated.

To Protest against the Policies of the Post-exilic Establishment?
First proposed by Bertholdt in 1816, this has long been a commonly held opinion. The story has been seen as a reaction against the prohibition on mixed marriages (and even enforced divorce) which formed part of the programme of Ezra and Nehemiah. However, it can be objected that the book is not at all polemical in tone, but rather positive. At 4.6 where a polemical tract might have made the point that the nearer kinsman does not refuse Ruth on grounds of race, no such point is made. Indeed the issue of Ruth's foreignness is considerably blunted by the way in which she at the outset embraces Yahweh as her God and Israel as her people. A further point is sometimes made, that the establishment would have been responsible for the inclusion of Ruth in the canon and cannot have felt itself to be especially criticized by the book. This, however, is a weak argument which assumes a simple polarity in the post-exilic community, such as is unlikely to have existed, and ignores the very great variety of the biblical canon as a whole, much of which really is polemical. Lacocque's hypothesis that Ruth is a novella subversive of the post-exilic hierocracy is subject to similar criticisms.

An interesting new variant on this line of approach has come from Michael Goulder, who has argued that Ruth can be understood as a kind of sermon preached on Deuteronomy 22–25, some of which is misunderstood (22.30; 25.5-10) and some covertly challenged (23.3-6). It could have begun from the activity of preaching on the Torah of Deuteronomy in the

Second Temple, when some of its legal provisions were already remote and not fully understood.

To Commend the Davidic Dynasty?

If it can be assumed that the genealogies are original, then it can be argued that the book primarily wishes to record the maintenance of a male line. David's known Moabite ancestry is glossed over by Judaizing his Moabite great-grandmother. Thus Hubbard (pp. 39-46; cf. Sasson, Gerleman), who argues on other grounds that Ruth dates from the early monarchical period suggests that it encourages popular acceptance of the Davidic dynasty by appealing to the continuity of Yahweh's guidance in the lives of Israel's ancestors and in particular of David's own ancestors. This purpose may also be evidenced in the number of parallels with Pentateuchal material that can be found in Ruth (Hubbard suggests eighteen in all), although the argument then encounters problems over the dating of the Pentateuch. The early monarchical period was a period in which a number of small neighbouring peoples were incorporated into the political kingdom of Israel, apparently without rancour, just as in Ruth, and it may be significant that the women in 4.14 proclaim the significance of the newborn Obed for Israel, not only for Judah; this, Hubbard suggests, would well fit a date of composition in the reign of Solomon, when the issue of the fitness of the house of David to rule over Israel was very much an issue. A compatible piece of work by Vuilleumier regards the original story as Davidic but as overlaid by later allegorizing in which Ruth is presented as a type of Israel returning from the Exile.

This line of argument does, of course, depend very heavily on the correct identification of the date of composition and on the questionable originality of the genealogical material in 4.17, 18-22.

To Provide a Window into the Reality of Women's Lives?

Very recent scholarship along feminist lines has raised a possible new function for Ruth, as a window into the positive reality of women's lives in the Old Testament period (e.g. Meyer), and so perhaps even as a text composed among women (picking up an older idea for which Campbell and others have argued). This is partly because of the choice of subject matter, the use of motifs of fullness and emptiness etc., but also because of the way the story is expressed (through dialogue, in large part, a technique that favours women because more than one point of view can be presented simultaneously and pregnant silences picked up by the attentive reader); and the way in which the woman Ruth is celebrated. In certain respects she takes on the roles that fairy tales often award to (male) heroes, leaving home to seek her fortune, and encountering hardships which she overcomes. In a particular scene which has overtones of other famous marriage stories in the Old Testament, a scene in which water is drawn for her, again Ruth takes the place of the bridegroom who in the other stories (e.g. that of Rebekah) has water drawn for him by a woman. Perhaps the story preserves a historical memory that women can benefit from the 'de-differentiation' of roles that tends to occur in times of crisis (so Berquist). The women in the story show solidarity to one another: they keep close to one another (*dābaq*, 'cleave'). Even the ancient title for God, El-Shaddai, which Naomi uses in 1.20-21 may be an allusion to God the Nurturer (from *šad*, 'breast') (see Cross, *Canaanite Myth*, pp. 55-56).

Feminists have their doubts about Ruth as a role model, however. She shows resourcefulness and practices *ḥesed* but she remains at least partly the outsider, the Moabite; nothing happens to improve the social system of Bethlehem, which could have left her in poverty. Boaz preserves her position in 4.5, 10 but thereafter she disappears. The key question whether women can represent the biblical God's point of view receives no less ambiguous an answer here than it does elsewhere. As the book ends, Naomi is acclaimed as the mother of Obed, while Ruth and Mahlon (the genealogy is of course solely interested in males) are left out. Some feminists would argue, even more negatively, that Ruth's very self-confidence is portrayed both as a strength and as a flaw: her sexual manipulativeness is, they say, only tolerated because she is not an Israelite but a Moabite, and cannot be fully incorporated into Israel. The very origins of Moab and

Ammon according to biblical tradition were due to sexual manipulativeness, and this, it is argued, is a trait which the Judaeo-Christian tradition has always found fascinating but always pushes to the margins of consideration.

Is Ruth erased or affirmed? Ultimately this is a matter of opinion formed on the basis of the reader's own contribution to determining the meaning of the text—and so is the significance of the answer. To hazard an answer, it is proper to consider the interests of women in studying any biblical text and to insist that they no longer be ignored, as was customary in the past. Yet a theology that is interested solely in the interests of women is too narrow to be of lasting significance, and an approach that seeks solely to 'deconstruct' a text by revealing all its hidden shortcomings can fall into the trap of ignoring what is good in it. This is not a helpful approach for the building up of the church.

To Commend the Practice of *ḥesed*?

It is the view of the rabbis that the purpose of Ruth is 'to teach how great is the reward of those who do deeds of kindness' (*Ruth R.* 2.13). This is certainly a key theme of the book; and perhaps the rabbis have correctly identified the one function of Ruth that most clearly transcends its original setting. It is a tribute to the author that the work is so difficult to confine to a particular era.

For Further Reading

In addition to essays in the *Feminist Companion* see:

J.L. Berquist, 'Role Dedifferentiation in the Book of Ruth', *JSOT* 57 (1993), pp. 23-37.

A. Phillips, 'The Book of Ruth—Deception and Shame', *JJS* 37 (1986), pp. 1-17.

René Vuilleumier, 'Stellung und Bedeutung des Buches Ruth im alttestamentlicher Kanon', *TZ* 44 (1988), pp. 193-210.

On Themes and Theology of Ruth:

N. Glueck, *Hesed in the Bible* (trans. A. Gottschalk; Cincinnati: Hebrew Union College Press, 1967).

R.L. Hubbard, 'Theological Reflections on Naomi's Shrewdness', *TynBul* 40 (1989), pp. 283-92.

W.S. Prinsloo, 'The Theology of the Book of Ruth', *VT* 30 (1980), pp. 330-41.

Esther

7

IS ESTHER THEOLOGICALLY VALUABLE?

> It is the duty of every man to drink at Purim until he cannot tell 'Blessed be Mordecai' from 'Cursed be Haman'! (*b. Meg.* 7a).

The book of Esther has often been viewed with suspicion both by Christians and by Jews, but above all by Christians. The story it tells may not be familiar and may seem outlandish on first sight. Briefly, it goes as follows. The setting is the court of the Persian king Ahasuerus at Susa. He is given to holding extravagant drinking parties, and during one of these he commands his queen Vashti to appear before his guests so that everyone can admire her beauty. Vashti refuses to come. There is instant consternation as the king and his sages picture all the women of Persia following her example. Hastily it is agreed that the king should make a royal decree 'written among the laws of the Persians and the Medes so that it may not be altered' (1.19) banishing Vashti from his presence and declaring that 'every man should be master in his own house' (1.22). The search is then on for a replacement for Vashti, and it is agreed that the best thing will be to hold a beauty contest and to make the winner the new queen.

At this point we are introduced to Esther, a beautiful Jewish orphan who has been brought up by her cousin Mordecai. He is an official at the Persian court, and makes it his business to enter Esther for the contest, counselling her 'not to reveal her people or kindred' (2.10). In due course, Esther wins the contest and becomes queen. She sets the seal on her victory by informing the king of a conspiracy against his life which Mordecai has overheard, and when the rumour is investigated and found to be true the conspirators are hanged and Mordecai's loyalty is 'recorded in the book of the annals' in the presence of the king.

Events are about to take an unfavourable turn, however, because the king promotes Haman, an Agagite (that is, an Amalekite, a traditional enemy of the Jews) (1 Sam. 15.7-9) to the office of grand vizier, an office which entitles him to the obeisance of all lesser officials—except that Mordecai, of course, refuses to bow to him, and thus earns the man's enmity. Haman's solution is extreme: he knows that Mordecai is a Jew, and he resolves to destroy not Mordecai alone but all the Jews throughout the whole kingdom of Ahasuerus (3.6). He will have a pogrom.

Arrangements are made in an appallingly ritualized way. 'They cast Pur—which means "the lot"—before Haman for the day and for the month, and the lot fell on the thirteenth day of the twelfth month, which is the month of Adar' (3.7). And Haman justifies his desires to the king by arguing that the Jews have laws 'different from those of every other people, and they do not keep the king's laws, so it is not appropriate for the king to tolerate them' (3.8). The king is persuaded, and an irrevocable decree goes out that on the appointed day all the Jews should be destroyed and their goods plundered. Their only hope lies in the faint possibility that Esther can intercede for them with the king, but it is thirty days since she was last summoned to the royal presence, it seems she has been forgotten, and to go unsummoned is an offence carrying the death penalty (4.11).

The story turns on the fact that Esther is nevertheless prepared to go. Supported by a fast specially called among the entire Jewish community in Susa, she achieves an audience with the king, and begins to work on him with some subtlety, having private banquets held for Ahasuerus, Haman and herself, and not stating her real request. Haman's delight at this apparent sign of royal favour makes him all the more eager to get rid of Mordecai without waiting for the pogrom which is not due for some months, so he plans to have Mordecai hanged in advance and builds an immense gallows, anticipating the king's permission (5.12-14).

But that night the king cannot sleep and resorts to having the royal annals read to him. Quite by chance—or is it providence?—he is reminded both that Mordecai once saved his life, and that he had never rewarded him for it. Accordingly, next day, he consults Haman about how best to reward 'the man whom the king wishes to honour' (6.8), and Haman, jumping to the conclusion that he is the fortunate man, suggests a triumphal procession through the city. He is mortified to discover his mistake.

This is the beginning of the end for Haman and his plans, for Esther is about to reveal to the king that she is one of the people who should be destroyed under Haman's pogrom. Ahasuerus seems to have forgotten that this was ever authorized, and the news fills him with wrath. Haman then seals his own fate by literally throwing himself upon Esther, in the king's absence, to beg for mercy, so that when the king suddenly enters the room Haman appears to be in a compromising position. Inevitably, he is hanged on the gallows he had intended for Mordecai, and Mordecai is made grand vizier in his place.

The edict concerning the pogrom cannot be revoked, but instead a second edict is issued allowing the Jews to defend themselves when the appointed day comes. As a result, no Jew dies; but 500 of their enemies are killed in Susa, and a further 75,000 in the provinces, and Haman's ten sons are hanged at Esther's special request. The Jews are finally enjoined by Mordecai always to keep the anniversary of the pogrom as a feast, to be called 'Purim' after the lot (Pur) originally cast to fix the date.

It is easy to see why this story has always had a mixed reception. On the one hand it deals with the deep-seated and historically justified fear the Jews have that they will be hated and persecuted because 'their laws are different from those of every other people'. It ill behoves Christians to object that in the story the Jews are shown rising above the threat. On the other hand, it is a fact that the ending of the story seems to glorify violence against the Gentiles, and that all the principal characters behave in ways that are morally or religiously questionable (Esther embraces a life in which she cannot possibly keep the Jewish law; Mordecai courts disaster by his disdain for Haman; the king is shallow and suggestible in the extreme, and so on). In addition, the book of Esther is the only one in the Bible in which God is never mentioned, and indeed no religious observance except fasting is mentioned either. The result is to make Judaism appear ethnic and no more.

Canonicity

Esther was accepted into the Jewish canon no earlier than the Council of Jamnia in AD 90, and perhaps not until the academy of Ousha met in 140; its acceptance may even be as late as AD 200. It was not accepted without difficulty, and arguments about its holiness continued to appear in the codification of oral law, known as the Talmud, down to the third century (*b. Meg.* 7a). These arguments centred on the fact that Esther did not 'defile the hands'. The use of the word 'defile' in this context is unexpected in modern parlance, but in ancient times holiness was conceived of almost as tangible and as capable of transference to the hands if a holy object such as a sacred scroll was touched; in this case the hands were said to be 'defiled'. So, if the Esther scroll was said not to defile the hands, that implied that it was not holy. Since the same objection was raised to at least two of the other five scrolls read at major festivals (known collectively as the Megilloth or 'scrolls') it seems that this late collection represents some kind of frontier in the Old Testament (so Clines, *Esther*). The judgment that the scroll might not defile the hands is of course a matter of psychology as well as intellect, and seems to have been based on recognition of the problems we have outlined above, plus the fact that canonical books were also required to be early in date (Esther is one of the latest books in the Old Testament), and orthodox in teaching. Orthodoxy is established if the work is consistent with the Torah (i.e. the first five books of the Bible, also known as the Pentateuch), and here the problem for Esther is that it authorizes a festival which is unknown to the Torah. None of these problems is, however, insurmountable: the story does contain positive qualities and does assume that the Jews are

God's people and that God has control of events (4.14); the Mishnah (an early part of the Talmud devoted to the codification of oral law) suggests that it is because the book of Esther sanctions merrymaking that the name of God is omitted, so that it cannot be inadvertently profaned; and the fact that Esther is linked to a popular festival has in the long run proved an advantage.

Taken as a whole, rabbinic tradition is strongly positive about Esther herself and makes her one of the seven female prophets of Israel (with Sarah, Miriam, Deborah, Hannah, Abigail and Huldah), appealing to Est. 5.1 ('she clothed herself in royalty') as evidence that she put on the Holy Spirit, and received divine inspiration.

Clear evidence of the popularity the book achieved is found in the fact that manuscripts of it are very abundant. It appears in all the complete private Bible codices, it is appended to the Torah in most synagogue scrolls, and appears with the other festival lections in liturgical scrolls. In addition, every Jewish family wants a copy in the manuscript form which the Talmud says should be read at Purim, and the result is that huge numbers exist, many of them very beautiful examples of the calligrapher's art. It is the only biblical book other than the books of the Torah on which more than one Targum (an interpretative translation from the original Hebrew into the more popular Aramaic) has been prepared; and unusually both the Jerusalem and Babylonian versions of the Talmud contain a running commentary on Esther. In fact, the Talmud comes very close to tracing the institution of Purim back to Moses by relating Exod. 17.14, 'The LORD said to Moses...I will utterly blot out the remembrance of Amalek from under heaven' to the statement in Est. 3.1 that Haman was an Agagite (which means an Amalekite); and the saying in Deut. 31.18, 'I will surely hide (*astîr*) my face', is held to imply that Esther will redeem Israel at a time when God hides his face (*b. Ḥul.* 139b). Indeed the great medieval Jewish philosopher Maimonides (d. 1204) declared that although the Prophets and Writings should pass away when the Messiah came, yet Esther and the Law should remain.

Within the Christian tradition, Esther has had an even

harder process of reception, since it has no function in the Christian liturgical year, and Christians have not identified with the experience of being ethnically Jewish (one wonders how differently Esther might have been received if it had spoken on behalf of 'Israelites' rather than 'Jews'!). On the contrary, Christians have suspected that they are representative of the gentiles against whom the book was written, and have become disapproving of its ethic of retribution. Esther was received in the Western church at the Council of Carthage in AD 397, but only with the apocryphal Additions (see Chapter 9 below), six passages added to the Hebrew text by the Alexandrian Jews who translated the book into Greek, and intended to remedy the lack of religious references in the original. In the Eastern church the book was received only in the eighth century. In contrast to the popularity of the book in Jewish tradition, in Christendom very little attention was paid to it from the New Testament down to the Reformation, and Luther complained 'I am so hostile to this book that I wish it did not exist, for it Judaïzes too much, and has too much pagan perversity' (*Table Talk*, W.A. xxii,2080) (cf. Paton, Esther in 1908, 'It should never have been included in the canon of the Old Testament').

A further development occurred at the Reformation in the Western church, when the apocryphal Additions to Esther were removed at Luther's instigation as part of a movement to rediscover Scripture in its most pristine form. Since then, Christian Bibles in the Protestant and Anglican traditions have included the short Hebrew-based version of Esther in the Old Testament and have printed the Additions only among the Apocrypha (which contains Greek material found in the Septuagint but surplus to the contents of the Hebrew Old Testament). It is not often realized that a change to the canon of the Old Testament has in fact been made so recently, albeit only in those churches which accept the Reformation.

Modern Reactions to Esther

In this century, both Jews and Christians have reassessed their reactions to Esther, with the result that an unexpected rapprochement may be taking place. On both sides, more attention has been paid to the literary genre of the work, which is no longer thought to be a piece of pure history (see Chapter 8 below).

On the Jewish side, Greenstein has mounted a spirited defence of Esther by explaining how it functions in the Jewish liturgical year, implicitly disapproving its abstraction from that context. It should be judged on its positive qualities, not on its negative characteristics which become more apparent outside of that context.

A more subtle approach is taken by Goldman, who has pointed out that although Jewish and Christian readers have disagreed as to whether Esther is ethical or not, neither side has paid much attention to the author's possible use of irony—a question which has important implications for the interpreter. Certainly Esther is full of 'rhetorical irony', such as the plot reversal whereby Haman is hanged on the gallows he had built for Mordecai, but Goldman argues that it also generates an ironical attitude in the reader ('generative irony'), prompting him or her to question the attitudes and assumptions that are being portrayed. For example, the fact that the Jews are given permission to massacre their enemies (8.11) has long troubled commentators, who have tried to argue either that the Jews only attack those who attack them (Gordis; but the Jews still kill over 75,000 men, according to 9.5); or that this is poetic justice required by the story-line (Clines, *Esther*); or that it is rough humour (Jones; although one wonders if such a comic safety-valve is ethically harmless). Goldman, presuming a Jewish readership, sees the significance of 8.11 in quite different terms: it shows Jews and Persians behaving alike, and this, he says, is highly ironical and leads to 'a bold questioning of the Jewish self-image' which is a highly ethical act. What is not so clear is whether the original author intended such irony (Goldman calls such an intention 'intuitive irony'); it is possible that he did not, but one cannot prove it, though there are other scholars who have called Esther a sapiential satire. In any case, it is a well established principle of literary criticism, whether biblical or secular, that the author's intentions cannot entirely circumscribe the meaning of the text and that the reader makes a crucial contribution to determining its meaning. At the extreme, however, some Jewish voices have been raised against Esther. In 1938, Shalom Ben-Chorin urged the abandonment of the festival of Purim and the banishment of Esther from the canon, as 'unworthy of a sacrificial people'.

It is paradoxical that simultaneously some Christian scholars are becoming more appreciative of Esther. It is true that critical voices continue to be raised, both on old grounds and on new ones. Thus Mosala, a black South African scholar, objects that the book does not question the Persian feudal system but 'aspires only to survival' or at best to some degree of influence within that system, and that it entirely subsumes gender struggle to this nationalist and survivalist programme: 'South African women cannot consent to the claim that such a biblical text supports them in their struggle'. Similarly the sociologist Norman Gottwald points out that even the statements that the Jews undertook 'no looting' (9.10, 15, 16) support a feudal ideology in which property assumes greater importance than people, and the choice of a female character to achieve such ends could be objectionable to women.

It is clear that these interpreters are raising objections which can be raised to a greater or lesser extent against any biblical text, given the changes in sociological assumptions that have occurred in the two thousand years and more since these texts were written. The authority of a sacred text that does not reflect one's life experience to a sufficient degree is going to become questionable (Fewell). But is it true that a text produced in a hierarchical, patriarchal society need be rejected automatically as 'unredeemable words of subjugation'? Fewell, herself a feminist scholar, would argue to the contrary, noting, for example, how in the case of Esther the author mocks the fragility of male sovereignty in the Vashti episode that opens the book. The text may stand for values which are timeless, such as the honouring of Esther's decision to plead for her people at the possible cost of her life, and Wilfrid Cantwell Smith in *What is Scripture?* has recently pointed out that in former ages of biblical interpretation it would have been assumed that the highest and best possible interpretation of the text was the right one, since any lesser interpretation would have been dishonouring to God who was the presumed inspiration of the text. (He adds, pointedly, that if this had not been the case biblical studies would not enjoy either the standing or the funding that they do enjoy in modern universities).

Interestingly, however, Esther is also gaining support from Christians who are beginning to appreciate and identify with its championship of the oppressed. Christians, in other words, are both beginning to show imaginative sympathy for the plight of the Jews, and to feel similarly stigmatized themselves. Put bluntly, Esther deals with fear by creating a story which resembles at some points the fear and anxiety in the audience, and by allowing them to see that fear played out on an objective stage it has therapeutic value: even if the fear remains, it has been 'named'. The comment of Matthew Henry who wrote in 1704 that Esther illustrated Ps. 37.12, 'The wicked plot against the righteous', now looks less isolated within Christian tradition. In the aftermath of the Second World War B.W. Anderson wrote that the book dramatizes 'the eternal miracle of Jewish survival' in the face of anti-Semitism. McCarthy (*The OT Short Story*) acknowledges that this story of threat and anxiety is intended to help the audience cope with their own fear and anxiety, and Webb has argued that the modern Christian can recognize 'analogies of context'.

Christians cannot simply read Esther as if they were Jews, however, because as Anderson perceived 'Esther raises the profoundest question, viz. the meaning of the election of Israel'—the scandal of particularity. It is not good to see the savage retribution pictured in Esther as the long-term solution (or even as an interim solution) to the tensions caused by this particularity. Rather, Anderson suggests that instead of entering into the situation Esther describes we should try to stand back from it and see, retrospectively, that God has kept Israel alive for his salvific purposes regardless of her merits or demerits, as an action of undeserved grace. This holds true whether one conceives of Israel as the Jewish community, the Christian community, or both. 'Christ both unites inseparably and draws the sharpest cleavage between the old and new covenants.'

This somewhat detached view is not, however, representative of more recent scholarship on Esther, particularly within the liberation theology movement, which emerged in the 1960s in Latin America (and has attracted the interest and support of both Jews and Christians). Craghan discussed the place of Esther in liberation theology in 1982, noting that Esther liberates herself by liberating others. (It is interesting that the two biblical books named after women, namely Ruth and Esther, plus the apocryphal book of Judith, have all been claimed as liberation texts, though each offers a slightly different paradigm of liberation. Craghan compares and contrasts them all.)

It is a fundamental conviction of liberation theology not only that the starting point for theological reflection is the liberation of the poor, but also that *orthodoxy must be accompanied by orthopraxis*. Orthodoxy (correct doctrine) is seen to be important but without orthopraxis (right action) there may be little one can say about sound doctrine. From this point of view, it matters very little that God is not specifically mentioned in Esther, provided that He is made known—as He is—in and through the events it describes. From the point of view of Hispanic Americans (Latin Americans who live as a minority in north America) Esther is deeply meaningful for three reasons (Costas). First, she remembered her roots and did not become wholly assimilated to Persian society, even though she offered it her loyal support. The book offers hope and support for the many minorities who wish to live this way in modern pluralistic societies. Secondly, she remembered her true vocation. It is easy for the Christian vocation to become deformed by conforming too much to the dominant system, so that the Church does not speak out against injustice or oppression, or makes feeble protests from the sidelines and remains practically inactive. Thirdly, Esther remembered God: this is seen as the well-spring of all her positive actions, and as the guarantee of her long-term prosperity (Jer. 22.15-16). Secular humanism may be less of a threat to faith than a lack of radical obedience among Christians to the declared will of God in the face of social or political opposition.

Costas acknowledges that Christians have been uneasy

about the ethnic particularity and indeed about the incipient feminism in Esther, but argues in contrast to Anderson that all victims can identify with the Jews in the story—and conversely that Jewish oppressors (visiting injustice on the Palestinians and Lebanese) cannot rightly claim this story as their own. Citing the names of Jewish soldiers who have faced prison sentences for refusing to fight on these fronts, he concludes that the memory of Esther (and Mordecai) 'can only be claimed in faithfulness to the cause of justice, in solidarity with the victims of injustice, and in daring obedience to the God who stands on the side of the poor, the powerless and the oppressed'. There is value in the modern 'hermeneutic of suspicion', but it must be complemented by a 'hermeneutic of hope'.

In fact, it has recently been noticed that although the story overtly satirizes Persian law it also implicitly condemns a way of thinking about law which has from time to time characterized both Judaism and Christianity, namely that it is something that can never be changed—even when changed circumstances make its contents obviously problematic. As Fewell says, Esther elbows into the fixed provisions of the Torah to make room for the new holiday of Purim, and in so doing keeps the canon from stagnating and becoming as problematic as the laws of the Medes and Persians.

For Further Reading

B.W. Anderson, 'The Place of the Book of Esther in the Christian Bible', *JR* 30 (1950), pp. 32-43 (= Moore, *Studies*, pp. 130-41).

O.E. Costas, 'The Subversiveness of Faith: Esther as a Paradigm for a Liberating Theology', *Ecumenical Review* 40 (1988), pp. 66-78.

J.F. Craghan, 'Esther, Judith and Ruth: Paradigms for Human Liberation', *BTB* 12 (1982), pp. 11-19.

D.N. Fewell, 'Feminist Reading of the Hebrew Bible: Affirmation, Resistance and Transformation', *JSOT* 39 (1987), pp. 77-87.

S. Goldman, 'Narrative and Ethical Ironies in Esther', *JSOT* 47 (1990), pp. 15-31.

R. Gordis, 'Studies in the Esther Narrative', *JBL* 95 (1976), pp. 43-58.

E.L. Greenstein, 'A Jewish Reading of Esther', in *Judaic Perspectives on Ancient Israel* (ed. J. Neusner; Philadelphia: Fortress Press, 1987), pp. 225-43.

B.W. Jones, 'Two Misconceptions About the Book of Esther', *CBQ* 39 (1977), pp. 171-81.

A. Lacocque, *The Feminine Unconventional: Four Subversive Figures in Israel's Tradition* (Minneapolis: Fortress Press, 1990).

I.J. Mosala, 'The Implications of the Text of Esther for African Women's Struggle for Liberation in South Africa', *Ideological Criticism of Biblical Texts*, *Semeia* 59 (1992), pp. 129-37.

B. Webb, 'Reading Esther as Holy Scripture', *RTR* 52 (1993), pp. 23-35.

S.A. White, 'Esther a Feminist Model for the Jewish Diaspora', in P.L. Day (ed.), *Gender and Difference in Ancient Israel* (Minneapolis: Fortress Press, 1989), pp. 161-77.

8

ESTHER
IS IT HISTORICAL?

IS THE ESTHER STORY history or fiction? Until the eighteenth century this was not a live issue: it was assumed that the events described were historical. Then Semler in 1773 suggested that the story was more in the nature of a romance—a suggestion much in line with the scientific spirit of the Enlightenment—and this is the view that has largely prevailed since. Important 'Introductions' to the Old Testament by Eissfeldt and Pfeiffer, for example, describe Esther as a historical novel and, as Clines (*Esther*) has argued, it is not satisfactory to gloss over this issue by saying (as Myers did in *The World of the Restoration*, 1968) that the accent is more on the adjective 'historical' than on the noun 'novel'. A novel is by definition a work of fiction, and to describe a novel as historical is merely to say that it is decked out with historically plausible details. A claim to historicity must be based on a higher degree of correspondence with externally verifiable events than that. (The 'annals of the kings of Media and Persia' mentioned as an independent source in 10.2 are unknown to us, and are unlikely to have been any more than a Jewish midrashic source.)

However, it would be wrong to give the impression either that Esther does not stand up well to certain kinds of verification, or that scholars are all of one mind in the conclusions they draw. The arguments for and against the historicity of Esther can be summarized as follows.

Arguments in Favour of Historicity

There are three main lines of argument in favour of the historicity of Esther, namely (1) that it is supported by the accounts of ancient historians, principally Herodotus (*History of the Persian Wars*, Books 7-9); (2) that it is supported by the findings of archaeology, particularly at the ancient Persian capital of Susa where the story is set; and (3) that the existence of Mordecai in particular becomes plausible in the light of ancient epigraphic evidence.

1. The Evidence of Ancient Historians

First, it should be explained that although the Jewish historian Josephus, who was a contemporary of Christ, thought that the monarch Ahasuerus was the king known to the Persians as Artaxerxes I (465–424 BC), the decipherment early in this century of trilingual inscriptions found on Persian monuments has made it almost certain that Ahasuerus (the name in this form is Hebrew) can be identified with Xerxes (this is a Greek name corresponding to the Persian name Khshayarsha). Most of the statements made about Ahasuerus in Esther fit the events of Xerxes' reign (486–465 BC) and do not fit those of any other Persian monarch. Even his character agrees with the portrayal of him by Herodotus and other classical historians.

Intriguingly, Ezra 4.6 says that in the year of Ahasuerus's accession 'they wrote an accusation against the inhabitants of Judah and Jerusalem', and the context implies that this accusation had to do with the rebuilding of the temple, although that had in fact been completed much earlier, in 520 BC. Controversy did occur over the rebuilding of the city walls, but later under Artaxerxes I (Ezra 4.12). The chronological sequence at the opening of the book of Ezra is notoriously confused. The historian Morgenstern has suggested that in 486 BC, the year of Xerxes' accession, the Jews joined a rebellion led by Egypt against the Persians, which was not put down until 483. It is not possible, however, to demonstrate that this underlies the book of Esther.

The author correctly describes some Persian customs of the time (so far as they are known to us from other sources), such as the existence of a council of seven to advise the monarch, the use of a postal system in the empire, and so on. He even uses ten Persian terms for Persian objects (all from the language of government and trade) and some thirty-five quasi-Persian names, although the authenticity of these has come under fire (e.g. in Moore, *Esther*).

2 Macc. 15.36 specifies that the defeat of Nicanor by Judas Maccabeus should be commemorated each year on the 'thirteenth day of the twelfth month—which is called Adar in the Aramaic language—the day before Mordecai's day'. This certainly shows that the Diaspora festival which is the subject of Esther was accepted in Palestine at an early date, although under a different name, and it has been suggested that the essential historicity of Esther must be assumed if we are to explain the fact of the observance of the festival. None of this, however, really proves the historicity of the story that accompanies the festival; bearing in mind the problems concerning the acceptance of Esther into the canon it is more likely that the story was not believed or valued in some quarters, and that it was fabricated to justify and commend the observance by all Jews of a feast that was originally observed only by a certain community of Diaspora Jews around Susa, and had pagan roots.

2. The Evidence of Archaeology

There was indeed a royal palace at Susa (though it belonged to Artaxerxes Mnemon, not Xerxes). The French archaeologist Perrot who has excavated the gate and the square before it (4.6) was impressed by the accord between archaeological findings and the biblical account. Support has also been claimed from the finding of the Lachish cosmetic burner for the practice attested in 2.12-13 of perfuming the whole body and clothes. Such verisimilitude, however, is to be expected in any historical novel and is not in itself a guarantee of historicity.

3. The Name of Mordecai

In two articles which appeared between 1941 and 1943, the scholar A. Ungnad published a tablet of uncertain date and provenance, but probably from fifth century Borsippa (so

Clines, *Esther*), containing a reference to a finance officer called Marduka visiting Susa on a tour of inspection in the reign of Xerxes. This, he claimed, could be the biblical Mordecai. The suggestion has been taken up and approved by a number of scholars such as Gordis, Yamauchi and (more cautiously) by Moore (who noted that the existence of the biblical Mordecai could not actually be proved by such means) and Anderson (who was less interested in the historicity of Mordecai than in the fact that the name was attested for a human being, since it is also reminiscent of the name of the Babylonian god Marduk).

Clines, however, has objected that the tablet has been overinterpreted. It refers to Marduka only as some kind of administrator (his office is unspecified) belonging to the satrapy of Ushtannu, otherwise known to the Bible as the province of 'Babylon and Beyond the River', and does not specify that he personally visited Susa, but only that he received monies from Susa. Yamauchi has responded by accepting Clines's criticisms, which he reinforces by stating that a full survey of Persian and Elamite tablets from Persepolis at this date reveals the existence of at least four Mardukas! But he adds that his survey has also added verisimilitude to Esther by turning up parallels to other names it contains, such as those in 1.10, 14; 3.1 and 9.7-9. None of this can really remove the force of Clines's objection that fictitious characters usually do bear names attested for real people, so that the presence of a Marduka at Xerxes' court is not relevant to the historicity of Esther.

Arguments against Historicity

A preliminary distinction should be made between evidence that damages a claim to historicity and evidence that just points to fiction-like traits in Esther (Clines, *Esther*). There is much in Esther that is not corroborated by the classical historians. Vashti, Esther, Haman and Mordecai are nowhere mentioned. In fact, Xerxes' queen from the seventh to the twelfth year of his reign (Est. 2.16; 3.7) was Amestris (Herodotus, *Histories* 7.114; 9.112), daughter of a Persian general. And during part of this period Xerxes was away fighting his Greek wars, and was not in Susa at all. Esther is supposed to have arrived at court in 480 while Xerxes was still away. It may strain credulity that the Persian empire should have had two non-Persian viziers one after another as well as a non-Persian queen. And the author is sometimes incorrect about Persian laws and customs. In particular, the notion of a Persian decree being unalterable once promulgated is not attested by any of the ancient historians, and its very impracticality in real politics makes its existence unlikely (Fox, *Character and Ideology*).

The account of the origin of Purim given in Esther is historically improbable. If the feast really originated in a historical event in Persian times and was accepted into the Jewish calendar in Persian times it is remarkable that it is not mentioned in the late Priestly strand of biblical law. Furthermore the word 'Purim' is neither Hebrew nor Persian and the meaning 'pur' = 'lot' suggested for it in 3.7 and 9.26 seems arbitrary; the plural form 'purim' is not accounted for. In fact, all the occurrences of the word in the book (3.7 and 9.20–10.3) could be secondary.

There are some historical implausibilities which can be explained away. For example, although it was until recently often objected, following Herodotus, that a Persian king could not have had a foreign queen because he would have been required to seek a wife within one of seven prominent Persian families, Clines has shown that a survey of who the Persian queens actually were does not support the existence of such a restriction. At first sight Est. 2.5-6 seems to say that Mordecai had been one of the Jews deported from Jerusalem in the time of Jeconiah, which would have made him 120 years old when the story opens—unless the text means (on a rather less natural reading of the Hebrew) that Mordecai's grandfather Kish was the deportee.

More serious is the question whether it is plausible that Xerxes authorized the extermination of the Jews, or that, having done so, he should have announced the massacre eleven months in advance. It has to be remembered that although pogroms are known to both ancient and modern historians (and even a delay of four months is instanced by Gordis) this slaughter of Jews by Persians is no more or less likely than the slaughter of Persians by Jews which is also a feature of the book, and which is also unknown to history.

As Clines emphasizes, we should not overlook the fact that the book does have notably novelistic qualities, such as the very frequent use of hyperbole, and that (even though it appears to be a tightly knit account, with no secondary material in the main body of the story), the author is indifferent to internal inconsistencies such as the fact that Esther hides her Jewishness yet Mordecai who is known to be a close relative does not. It is a romantic story, like Daniel 1–6, Tobit, Judith, and Ahikar. With its location in an exotic court, its constant banquets, its extravagance, its bloodshed and its constantly plotting courtiers (and even with its reversal of the expected disaster for the underdogs) it has a strong flavour of the Arabian Nights. Even the opening words have an air of 'once upon a time' about them.

While therefore it is not impossible that Esther has an historical core, it is very improbable—especially in view of the literary characteristics of the book—that it is primarily an historiographic work. It has much authentic colouring, but maybe no more than one should expect from a historical novel. Fox reckons that the author intended his work to have verisimilitude, since historicity was desirable in order to underpin the celebration of Purim and to ensure its acceptance in the canon; he did, in short, want his book to be classed with the works attributed to Ezra, Nehemiah and the Chronicler (cf. Clines, Myers), and this self-presentation as history is not necessarily falsification. What, in any event, is history? As Halpern points out in *The First Historians*, anyone can present material which contains distortion (unwitting or otherwise) as 'history' and still be engaged in history writing. The ancient author of Esther may not have realized that he was leaving any clues to enable the modern historian to judge him unhistorical. Any real historical core in Esther is likely to be, in Clines's words, 'very tiny'. Rather, Esther is best understood as a typological treatment of anti-Semitism.

What is the Real Origin of Purim?

This question is fully discussed by Paton in his ICC commentary, and his discussion is still of interest as so little solid fresh evidence has come to light.

It has been argued that the origin of Purim must be Jewish because its admission to the calendar is otherwise hard to explain. Thus Michaelis in 1772 suggested that it referred to the victory of Judas Maccabeus over the Syrian general Nicanor (1 Macc. 7.39-50; 2 Macc. 15.20-36 etc.), and that the name Purim is derived from the word 'pura' meaning winepress, as an allusion to the crushing of the grapes of wrath by the victors. But this etymology has been severely criticized, and the theory faces several serious problems namely (a) that the Maccabean victory was celebrated on 13th Adar whereas 'Mordecai's day' was apparently already established at that time as a feast on 14th-15th Adar (confirmed among others by Josephus, *Ant.* 11.292); (b) the theory cannot account for the prominent role given to a woman in the story; and (c) no reason is given for the connection of a Persian story with a Jewish event having an entirely different meaning. Paton rightly observes that a feast with a truly Jewish origin would have a true story to go with it, whereas one from a pagan origin would have a fiction such as Esther appears to be.

Another possibility which has long been discussed is that Esther has older Gentile material standing behind it, and perhaps relates to the Persian New Year festival held at the spring (vernal) equinox. The word Purim, which has never been successfully related etymologically to any Hebrew term, could then derive from an old Persian equivalent of the Vedic *purti* 'portion' in the sense of 'gift', originally denoting the gifts exchanged at the festival and now reflected in the gifts Jews give to each other at Purim (9.19). One could envisage Diaspora Jews adopting such a feast on a secular basis, as a holiday, in much the same way as they have adopted Christmas in more recent times. Alternatively, it could be a disguised feast of all souls, which took up the last ten days of the Persian year, and was marked by making offerings to the dead. Adar is especially associated with the commemoration of the dead (Moses, Elijah and Miriam are all said to have died in this month, and Jewish graves are whitewashed at this time, a custom which can be traced back to Persia). Two of the Greek Additions to Esther (Additions A and F, see Chapter 9 below) certainly make history out of Persian mythology by using motifs centrally connected to the Persian New Year festival (Hutter). The festival is supposed to be a post-battle day of pleasure (9.19) and therefore perhaps mirrors seasonal rites such as conflict, which were part of the duality of ancient Iranian society (Gaster, *Purim and Hanukkah*, 1960) However, the dates of neither the Persian feast for the dead, nor of the New Year festival precisely coincide with those of Purim, and religions are notoriously conservative in such matters.

A further question arises as to whether the origins of Purim can be traced back behind the rise of the Persian empire into the period of the Babylonian empire which preceded it. Geographically this is entirely plausible, as Susa and Babylon are both located in eastern Mesopotamia, and in view of the mythology that has come down to us from that vanished world the theory gains in plausibility. The main characters in the book of Esther can be equated with the gods and goddesses of ancient Babylon and Elam (a kingdom directly to the east of Babylon in the mountainous region now separating Iraq from Iran). The names of Mordecai and Esther, who are cousins, sound comparable to those of Marduk, the Babylonian high god, and his companion Ishtar—the Babylonian Venus—who was his cousin. Hama was an Elamite solar deity and Vashti could be an Elamite goddess. Some of the symbolism applied to the characters in Esther and in Jewish interpretative tradition supports the hypothesis. Bearing in mind that Susa was on the boundary between ancient Babylon and Elam, it is possible that local tradition retained a memory of rivalry between these old deities, and of wars between their devotees.

The theory breaks down on the fact that there is no single myth or festival which runs parallel to the Esther story. There was a Babylonian *puhru* or assembly at which fates were determined for the coming year, and a feast was held, with an atmosphere of carnival misrule which the Jews as subject peoples could have enjoyed. But again the etymology is suspect and the feast is in the first two weeks of Nisan, which is the month after Adar. Furthermore, there is no role in it for an Esther. It is evident that, as Ringgren says, any borrowing that has taken place has been at best very indirect.

When was Esther Written?

The implication of 9.20-32, which was taken up by Clement of Alexandria and many other ancient scholars, both Jewish and Christian, was that Mordecai wrote the book soon after the events it describes. At all events, it was assumed that the book was roughly contemporaneous with those events. But a careful reading shows that 9.20 does not even purport to refer to the whole book, and it is strange that Esther is nowhere referred to before the Christian era, not even in Sirach (where the great passage 'let us now praise famous men' in chs. 44–49 omits both Esther and Daniel). The day of Mordecai is mentioned in 2 Macc. 15.36, and 1 Macc. 7.49 which is earlier has a similar but incomplete reference; it is Josephus who first cites the Greek version of Esther in *Apion* 1.8. There is no firm evidence that Purim was observed by Palestinian Jews before the first century bc. Furthermore, although the dating of biblical Hebrew is not an exact science, it has been thought throughout this century that the Hebrew of Esther is as late as any in the Old Testament, and that it contains many words not found elsewhere except in the Mishnah and other rabbinic writings. In addition, the intellectual standpoint of the book is late.

The question then is, how late? The argument put forward in the early part of this century that Esther dates from the Greek period and reflects in some way the struggles of the Maccabees has in the long run not found favour. Recently Horbury has published an instance of the use of the name 'Mardochaeus' (a Hellenized version of Mordecai) in a Jewish Egyptian tomb inscription of c. 150 BC, and suggests that this is evidence that something like the Esther story was already known there before the time of the Maccabees. Indeed as he also points out, the Maccabees are connected with the founding of the festival of Hanukkah, which has a very different timing and rationale to Purim.

In favour of a setting in the Persian period it has been suggested by Heltzer that the book was composed shortly after the suppression of a revolt in Judaea under Artaxerxes in 340 bc. Some Jewish scholars, following hints in rabbinic tradition, also argue that the conflict in Esther reflects tensions between repatriated Judaeans and Samarians in the Achaemenid period. There was a Susian element among the elite of Samaria, and both parties lobbied the Persian overlords in the Samarian capital.

The colophon to the Greek version of Esther suggests that the book was brought to Egypt no later than 73 BC, and perhaps earlier in 114 BC. It had originated either in Jerusalem or in the eastern diaspora (which is indirectly referred to in 3.8), and was translated into Greek in Maccabean Jerusalem to make it accessible to the whole diaspora. The text itself may preserve a memory that each community was originally independent in its observance of the feast, the eastern diaspora celebrating on 15 Adar and the Palestinians on 14 Adar, but that it eventually became ecumenical and lasted two days (Est. 9.21).

For Further Reading

D.J.A. Clines, 'In Quest of the Historical Mordecai', *VT* 41 (1991), pp. 129-36.

T. Gaster, *Purim and Hanukkah* (New York: Schuman, 1960).

R. Gordis, 'Studies in the Esther Narrative', *JBL* 95 (1976), pp. 43-58 (= Moore, *Studies*, pp. 408-23).

M. Heltzer, 'The Book of Esther—Where Does Fiction Start and History End?', *BARev* 8 (1992), pp. 24-30,41.

W. Horbury, 'The Name Mardochaeus in a Ptolemaic Inscription', *VT* 41 (1991), pp. 220-26.

M. Hutter, 'Iranische Neujahrfestmythologie und der Traum des Mordechai', *Biblische Notizen* 44 (1988), pp. 39-45.

J.C.H. Lebram, 'Purimfest und Estherbuch', VT 22 (1972), pp. 208-22 (= Moore, *Studies*, pp. 205-19).

C.A. Moore, 'Archaeology and the Book of Esther', BA 38 (1975), pp. 62-79 (= Moore, *Studies*, pp. 369-86).

H. Ringgren, 'Esther and Purim', *SEÅ* 20 (1956), pp. 5-24 (= Moore, *Studies*, pp. 185-204).

A. Ungnad, 'Keilinschriftliche Beiträge zum Buch Ezra und Esther', *ZAW* 58 (1940), pp. 240-44 (= Moore, *Studies*, pp. 356-60).

E.M. Yamauchi, 'Mordecai, the Persepolis Tablets and the Susa Excavations', *VT* 42 (1992), pp. 272-75.

—*Persia and the Bible* (Grand Rapids: Baker, 1990).

R. Zadok, 'On the Historical Background of the Book of Esther', *Biblische Notizen* 24 (1984), pp. 18-23.

9

ESTHER
THE TRADITION HISTORY

A SPECIAL FEATURE of Esther studies is the existence of substantially different versions of the book in the Hebrew and the Greek languages, attested from ancient times. In this chapter we will examine the relationship between these versions, taking the Hebrew text as the standard of comparison.

The Integrity of the Hebrew Text

There are very few textual variants in the standard Hebrew (or Masoretic) text of Esther: Paton's *Esther* lists twenty-nine, all of them trivial. This is unusual, and paradoxically may be due to the fact that Esther was the subject of so much controversy in the second century both within Judaism and (it can be conjectured) between Jews and Christians, that the need arose to have a fixed basis of discussion between rabbis, a basis that was then adhered to with great faithfulness.

What is not so clear is whether the Hebrew text as we now have it was or was not an authorial unity. Source critics have long been suspicious of the authenticity of 9.20–10.3 for several reasons: first, although the language of this section is similar to that of the rest of the book it contains a different selection of key phrases; secondly, it often contradicts other parts of the book (for example 9.29-32 has Esther writing a letter which largely duplicates Mordecai's letter in 9.20-23, and both of these letters require the Jews to hold the anniversary of the failed pogrom as a festival, even though 9.19 has already said that this became customary); and thirdly, 10.2 actually suggests the existence of a separate source, 'the annals of the kings of Media and Persia'. Thus 9.20-32 and 10.1-3 are often regarded as separate additions. Clines in his commentary goes further and treats the whole of ch. 9 regarding the vengeance of the Jews on their enemies as an addition which is not of a piece with the preceding chapters either linguistically or in terms of story line. The book would then have ended with the paradox of two mutually contradictory but unalterable royal decrees in existence, the one against the Jews and the other in their favour: 'the story thus reflected the irony of diaspora Judaism's position, both protected and threatened by the imperial powers to which it was subject'.

Yet it has to be admitted that the book would be incomplete for liturgical purposes without this material, which makes much more of the official institution of Purim than the rest of the book, and thus provides it with its major rationale. B.W. Jones would deny that the book lends itself to redaction criticism at all; and the rhetorical analysis of Berg makes a strong case in favour of the authenticity of 9.20–10.3.

The Septuagint and Additions

The most important Greek version of Esther is the one which is normally included in the Septuagint translation of the Old Testament (LXX), and for reasons which will appear later it is sometimes called the B-text. It is literarily stylish and faithful to the content rather than to the exact wording of the Hebrew—which it frequently condenses slightly—but overall it is 107 verses longer than the Hebrew version discussed above. The extra material occurs in six Additions customarily referred to by the letters A-F. The six Additions are customarily clustered together at the end of the book in Est. 10.4–16.24, rather than at their correct points in the story line, and their contents are (following Clines, *The Esther Scroll*):

A. (11.2–12.6) A dream of Mordecai concerning the coming destruction, and his discovery of the chamberlains' conspiracy [A should be prefixed to 1.1].
B. (13.1-7) The contents of the edict against the Jews sent out by Ahasuerus at Haman's instigation [B follows 3.13].
C. (13.8–14.19) Prayers of Mordecai and Esther for deliverance [C follows 4.17].
D. (15.1-16) An account of Esther's appearance before the king in anxiety for her own safety (an alternative account to 5.1-20) [D follows C].
E. (16.1-24) The contents of the edict on behalf of the Jews sent out by Ahasuerus at Mordecai's instigation [E follows 8.12].
F. (10.4–11.1) The interpretation of Mordecai's dream as relating to the events of the narrative [E follows 10.3].

Because the long Greek B-text was familiar to Christians it was long regarded as canonical by the Church, even though Jerome in his Latin translation of the Bible, the Vulgate, gathered up the long Additions and placed them together at the end of Esther in deference to the fact that he knew that they were absent from the Hebrew. Only at the Reformation did Protestantism remove them to the Apocrypha altogether, on the ground that canonicity required a Hebrew or Aramaic original; subsequently the Roman Catholic church decided at the Council of Trent (AD 1546) that although the Additions should strictly be regarded as 'deuterocanonical' they should still appear within the body of the Old Testament, after the basic text of Esther. This basic divergence between Protestant and Catholic-sponsored Bible translations still continues, but is eased by the fact that some modern translations such as the NRSV offer both an MT-based Esther in the body of the Old Testament, and a Septuagint (B-text) based Esther in the Apocrypha.

Both the B-text as a whole and the Additions in particular are designed to add religiosity to the text (a quality conspicuously lacking from the Hebrew but particularly evident in Addition C); to buttress its authenticity (B and E); to satisfy the reader's curiosity for more details, particularly about Mordecai; and to meet the reader's possible objections to points of difficulty in the original, such as Esther's apparently happy acceptance of foreign concubinage. Addition D is pure drama, about Esther's entry into the king's presence, but has less emphasis on her courage than on God's providence. The name of God, previously absent, now appears over fifty times (not only in the Additions but in the main text at 2.20; 4.8; and 6.1). Thus the B-text as a whole can be thought of as the first commentary on Esther.

Ironically, the material in the Additions which was designed to improve the book has been an important ground of complaint against it on the part of some Christian scholars who have noted that this material is, while unexpectedly sympathetic to Ahasuerus, still hostile to Gentiles in a generalized way—and in a way that the original story was not, making the Jew–Gentile controversy universal rather than particular. A separate commentary on the Additions has been provided by C.A. Moore, who concludes that they were both a symptom and a result of Esther's questionable status, that is, they were invented to remedy the book's deficiencies, but such large scale tampering was only admissible because the book's status was questionable. Moore's commentary is indispensable for work on the Additions, but has been criticized for interleaving them not with the B-text but with the Masoretic text; his intention was to point up the contrasts between them, but it has been objected that the result is too much of a hybrid.

The Greek Alpha Text

The Greek text of Esther in contrast to the Hebrew has been extremely unstable. The very fact that the standard Greek text is known as the B-text immediately reveals that there is also an A or alpha text (sometimes called 'Lucianic', though scholars no longer believe that it is connected with Lucian, the Christian scholar and martyr). Moore, Clines and Fox among others envisage the A-text, which contains a relatively short and economical telling of the Esther story, as a fairly close *translation of a variant Hebrew tradition*, either an ancestor or cousin of the Masoretic text, in which personal names, numbers, dates and repetitious elements in the MT story are 'omitted'. This is significant, because the missing elements include, for example, the assumption of the inalterability of Persian law, the authorization of a second day of fighting and celebration and the Purim aetiology. No Jew is likely to have sacrificed these elements from the story once they were present in it, and this means that the Masoretic text which has become the standard Hebrew version cannot simply be assumed to be 'the' version that left the pen of the original author (against Bardtke)! Confusingly, however, the A-text has in course of time absorbed the six Additions which originated in the B-text tradition, plus a secondary ending corresponding approximately to MT 8.17–10.3, plus a few other verses, and is now longer than the mt. Clines has helpfully supplied the only complete English translation of the A-text in his monograph *The Esther Scroll* (1984), which applies text criticism, source criticism, redaction criticism and literary criticism to establishing all the stages of growth (five are suggested) of the Esther tradition.

The Versions Compared

The chronological relationship between the different versions of Esther is highly complex, but if it could be established we would be able to observe the changes that the theology of the book underwent in the course of retelling. Useful summaries of the present state of discussion are provided in Fox, *Character and Ideology* (pp. 254-73), and Day, *Three Faces of A Queen* (pp. 226-32).

Very briefly, the hypothetical short Hebrew text which underlay the Greek A-text is probably as close as we can get to the fountainhead of the Esther tradition; it does not presuppose the inalterability of Persian law but resolves the crisis brought about by Haman's plotting simply by allowing the edict arranging the pogrom to be annulled at Mordecai's request; Jewish influence at court is the safeguard against Jewish vulnerability; and the deliverance is celebrated once. Esther herself has a low profile. Second in line is the Masoretic text which introduces a coherent set of changes designed to resolve the crisis by way of a counter-decree and the battles of Adar, and an elaborate dialectical process institutionalizing the annual holiday of Purim. Events seem to have a momentum beyond the king's control, and the Jews depend to a greater extent on communal effort to save themselves; the anniversary of their efforts is commemorated year by year as Purim is added to the Jewish calendar. In this story Esther has become stronger. Finally in the LXX (B-text) version the story has expanded again, and Clines has suggested that the effect of the Additions is 'to assimilate the book of Esther to a scriptural norm', especially as found in the Persian histories of Ezra, Nehemiah and Daniel. The intervention of God at critical moments, the use of dreams, prayers, the quoting of the decrees, are all features found in these histories. These are important new insights which have been accepted by Fox, for example. It is not, however, universally agreed that Clines's conclusions exhaust the significance of the Additions. Rather, Fox wishes to emphasize the impact of the introduction of religious themes which are at best only implicit in the Hebrew tradition: God is explicitly shown to be in control of history, and earthly reality will ultimately follow this 'hyper-reality'; man is able to obtain access to heavenly wisdom through dreams granted to the righteous (though dreams may give meaning to the past rather than predict the future)—and as for woman, Esther is more stereotypically feminine than in the mt; finally, the people of Israel have an increased role in the playing out of the cosmic drama. Individual characters have become less important than cosmic generalities, and the festival of Purim itself is de-emphasized. The story does not, of course, stabilize even at this point, for it continues to grow and be retold in every translation, midrash and literary re-creation.

Where did the versions originate? The texts themselves offer few direct clues. Although the end of Addition F (11.1) seems to refer to events of 114 BC or 73 BC, depending on one's interpretation of it, this may be an addition to the Addition; it could have been written in Egypt to commend Purim to Egyptian Jews by representing it as a festival endorsed by a Jerusalem priest. Charles Dorothy is one of the few people who has attempted to find a specific social context for each of the versions. He regards the B-text as relatively 'neutral', detached from the events it observes, and intended for a Hellenized diaspora audience. The writer of the A-text by contrast was writing for fellow-Jews, feels closer to the story and is more a part of its actions. He is less Hellenized and more orthodox than the writer of the B-text, and possibly even wrote in Palestine. However, Dorothy has been challenged because his conclusions depend on the accuracy of his characterizations of the versions, which are open to question. Thus Day and Fox believe that the A-text is really more tolerant of Gentiles than the B-text, and Day argues at some length that claims of more Jewishness and less Hellenism in the A-text are 'inaccurate and incomplete'; in Day's own view the A-text is best treated as a Jewish–Persian amalgam, a model for diaspora Judaism, while the B-text in contrast gives Esther greater affinity with the religious community, and could therefore be Palestinian! The Masoretic text holds the middle ground in which Jewish–Persian relations are good but coolly professional, and could come from anywhere. Further discussion of the literary differences between the three main versions will be found in Chapter 10 below.

By way of postscript to this discussion it should be mentioned that although no fragments of the canonical book of Esther have been found at Qumran (and significantly none of the liturgical calendars at Qumran include the festival of Purim), J.T. Milik has claimed to identify several fragments of an Aramaic proto-Esther [4QprEst ar] in the materials reclaimed from Cave 4. Attempting to fit these into the textual history of Esther, which he analyses at careful length, Milik concludes that the Masoretic text was itself translated from Greek—an unusual though not unprecedented suggestion—and originated shortly after the First Jewish War. Prior to this, Proto-Esther materials such as those represented in the Cave 4 fragments were circulating in Judaea and influenced the many variant traditions still extant. These proposals have yet to be fully absorbed into Esther studies.

For Further Reading

J.J. Adler, 'The Book of Esther—Some Questions and Responses', *JBQ* 19 (1990–91), pp. 186-90.
D.J.A. Clines, *The Esther Scroll: The Story of the Story* (JSOTSup, 30; Sheffield: JSOT Press, 1984), especially Part IV, 'A Sequence of Esther Stories'.
H.J. Cook, 'The A-text of the Greek Versions of the Book of Esther', *ZAW* 81 (1969), pp. 369-76.
L. Day, *Three Faces of a Queen: Characterization in the Books of Esther* (JSOTSup, 186; Sheffield: JSOT Press, 1995).
C.V. Dorothy, *The Books of Esther: Structure, Genre and Textual Integrity* (JSOTSup, 187; Sheffield: Sheffield Academic Press, forthcoming).
M.V. Fox, *The Redaction of the Books of Esther* (SBLMS, 40; Atlanta: Scholars Press, 1991).
B.W. Jones, 'The So-called Appendix to the Book of Esther', *Semitics* 6 (1978), pp. 36-43.
S.E. Loewenstamm, 'Esther 9.29-32. The Genesis of a Late Addition', *HUCA* 42 (1971), pp. 117-24 (= Moore, *Studies*, pp. 227-34).
R.A. Martin, 'Syntax Criticism of the LXX Additions to the Book of Esther', *JBL* 94 (1975), pp. 65-72 (= Moore, *Studies*, pp. 595-602).
J.T. Milik, 'Les modèles araméens du livre d'Esther dans la Grotte 4 de Qumrân', *RevQ* 15 (1991), pp. 321-406.
C.A. Moore, *Daniel, Esther and Jeremiah: The Additions* (AB, 44; New York: Doubleday, 1977), pp. 153-252.
—'Esther revisited Again: A Further Examination of Certain Esther Studies of the Past Ten Years', *HAR* 7 (1983), pp. 169-86.
—'A Greek Witness to a Different Hebrew Text of Esther', *ZAW* 79 (1967), pp. 351-58 (= Moore, *Studies*, pp. 521-28).
—'On the Origin of the LXX Additions to the Book of Esther', *JBL* 92 (1973), pp. 382-93 (= Moore, *Studies*, pp. 583-94).
C.C. Torrey, 'The Older Book of Esther', *HTR* 38 (1944), pp. 1-40 (= Moore, *Studies*, pp. 448-87).

10

ESTHER AS LITERATURE

IN THE INTRODUCTION we discussed the books of Esther and Ruth as examples of the short story genre, finding common ground perhaps in their joint comparison with the Joseph story in Genesis. Joseph and Esther are alike as exemplars of the same genre (together with Dan. 1–6 and Judith), the diaspora short story. But genres are never pure. To what extent does Esther partake of other genres? Can both Esther and Joseph be described as 'historicized wisdom tales'? Has the Joseph story influenced the precise content of Esther?

The Genre of Esther

Esther as Festival Lection

The present function of Esther is clearly as a festival lection. The primary requirement of the rabbinic Purim observance is to hear the reading of the scroll so that the community remembers its ancestors' experience. What is not so clear is whether the story was written as a 'festival aetiology', that is, as a narrative that explains the origin of the festival. Ringgren and Gerleman have argued that this is the case, but Meinhold argues that while this is the book's purpose, it is not its genre. Fox, however, argues that this purpose is intrinsic to the MT of Esther.

Esther Modelled on Exodus?

Another suggestive hypothesis which we owe to Gerleman has it that Esther was patterned after Exodus 1–12 and contains all its essential features: the setting at a foreign court, the mortal danger to the Jews, acts of deliverance and revenge, the triumph of the Jews over their foes, and the establishment of a festival (Passover). As with the Joseph story, it is possible to find more detailed comparisons than that: Esther and Moses are both adopted (Exod. 2.9; Est. 2.7) and keep their origins secret (Exod. 2.10; Est. 2.10, 20). Each narrative provides the hero with a spokesman (Esther for Mordecai, Est. 2.20; 4.8; 9.20-23; and Aaron for Moses, Exod. 4.15-16), and each portrays the Amalekites as the arch-enemies of Israel (Exod. 17.8-16). Both Esther and Moses have to appear repeatedly before the monarch to intercede for their people (Exod. 7.14–12.28; Est. 5.2; 7.2; 8.3). And the destruction of Israel's enemies in Est. 9.1-6 parallels the destruction of the Egyptians in the Exodus. Therefore it may be that Esther has adapted a central tradition of salvation history and adapted it to the diaspora situation by making it less overtly religious.

As with the Joseph comparison, closer inspection shows that Gerleman's proposal, intriguing though it is, can be pushed too far (Berg). For example, the comparison of Esther with Moses is surely in tension with the comparison also made of Esther with Aaron in her capacity as spokesperson for Mordecai. More generally, the two stories do not share the same attitude to the foreign court, nor do they deal with the same problems—a point that can be clearly seen by considering how different are the festivals, Passover and Purim, which are connected to these stories. Recent work by Nina Collins has shown that the elements in the Esther story to which Gerleman particularly appeals are not present in the Greek A-text which, as we have seen, is possibly an older version of the story than that in the Masoretic text, so that the Exodus comparison, so far as it goes, is a secondary overlay on the Esther story. Exodus, like Joseph, has exercised some influence on the book of Esther, but it is 'neither controlling nor pervasive' (Berg). One can at least agree with Clines that whether or not the author intended us to read Esther as a commentary on Exodus 1–12, the presence of both in the same canon now invites us to do so.

Esther a Historicized Wisdom Tale?
Talmon classified both Joseph and Esther as 'historical wisdom tales', appealing to (a) their shared concept of a rather remote deity, and corresponding anthropocentrism; (b) lack of interest in Jewish history or community; (c) use of static typological characters; and (d) the use of wisdom motifs such as that of the wicked man meeting a bad end (Prov. 26.27), or of a principal character being adopted by a wise man (not found in Joseph but arguably true of Esther and also featuring in Ahiqar). In this, Talmon built upon the insight of von Rad that the Joseph story 'illustrates the realization of wisdom precepts in practical life'. In addition, the motif of the 'wise courtier' may be a significant link (Humphreys), although it is not clearly present in Esther, where wise behaviour is split between both Esther and Mordecai (who foolishly refuses to bow to Haman, a not inconsiderable figure in his own right). But we have already seen that there are difficulties in regarding Esther as historical, and again it can be objected that once Talmon has plundered Esther for his purposes he has impoverished it and left it lacking any connection with Purim, which is arguably anticipated from the beginning of the book. There are important non-wisdom elements in Esther which have not been taken into account, and as ever there are problems in pinning down any literary theme or technique as peculiar to the wisdom tradition, even if it could appropriately be used there.

Fox undercuts this line of thought still further by insisting that strictly there are very few examples of the 'historicized wisdom tale' apart from the preamble to the Aramaic Ahiqar and the Egyptian (Demotic) Onchsheschonqy, and that most of the wisdom features Talmon claims to find in Esther are in fact more characteristic of didactic wisdom (i.e. Proverb-type literature). Even then, some of the features claimed are false: Proverbs mentions God repeatedly; Esther finds Jewish national history of central concern. What really unites stories like Joseph, Esther and indeed Daniel 1–6 is not so much wisdom as a 'palace intrigue' background.

The comparison with the Joseph story was first made by Rosenthal (1895) and has since been accepted by Gerleman,

Talmon, Humphreys and Bardtke. It is based not only on a general similarity in setting and events, whereby a Jew can rise from lowly status in a foreign country and use his or her position to save others (despite initially being a passive character, and despite being forgotten at a crucial moment), but also on the use of shared motifs such as two eunuchs who act against the king (Gen. 40.1-3; Est. 2.21-23), the king having troubled nights (Gen. 41.9-45; Est. 6.1-11), the banqueting scenes, the reversals of fortune, the hangings—and there are even some instances of parallel phrasing such as Gen. 41.42-43//Est. 6.11; Gen. 39.10//Est. 3.4; Gen. 44.34//Est. 8.6.

It can, however, be objected (e.g. Berg, Fox) that the similarities of phrasing are rather ordinary so that their force depends on valid comparisons of other kinds being made between the two texts, and that in fact the amount of weight given to the comparable themes and motifs varies greatly from story to story. Fox raises the serious objection that Joseph deals with voluntary exile in hard times—hardly something that the book of Esther wishes to advocate.

One further scholar should be mentioned in this connection. Meinhold has described the connection between Joseph and Esther as being due primarily to a shared structure, which, however, Esther puts to the service of a more secularized intellectual attitude stemming from its transmission in a different (i.e. diaspora) community. The difficulty with this thesis is that the structural units Meinhold identifies in Joseph are sometimes overlapping and non-successive, and it looks as though he has in practice imposed the structure of Esther on Joseph's story, which is the opposite move to the one he seeks to demonstrate (so Berg). Interestingly, the Joseph story, like the book of Esther, is not referred to elsewhere in the Bible. Perhaps, therefore, both are late, with Joseph being written between 650 and 425 BC, although this view would be controversial.

To sum up, it appears that Esther may be in some sense a reinterpretation of the Joseph story, but that the reasons are not clear and the divergences between the two are as important as the similarities. There is insufficient ground for describing either as a historicized wisdom tale.

Relation to Other Contemporaneous Literature

Linda Day and others have noted that Esther bears certain likenesses to Hellenistic novels or 'romances' in its structure, its interest in luxury, its satiric quality, its erotic concern with the Persian king's love-life and its portrayal of the heroine as a young, attractive victim, somewhat alone and at the mercy of impersonal controlling forces. Of course it is the Additions that move most toward these Greek norms, but even with the Additions the Esther story remains distinctively different from the 'romance' genre in that eroticism and adventure are not the dominant concerns in any of the versions.

Esther can also bear partial comparison with other Jewish literature of the same period, such as the books of Judith and Susanna, which are alike in tending to expand the roles of female characters; or Daniel 1–6, a comparison that Fox finds interesting because the two are though close in date still different enough not to have been produced by imitation or borrowing, so that one can deduce that both were shaped by something external to either—the attitudes and goals of their time.

Esther as Folklore

Finally it should be mentioned that Niditch cuts a way through the multifarious comparisons of Esther with other tales by suggesting that they are caused by the shared use of 'traditional style composition' which inhabits 'the gray area where idiom meets formula', and is typical of folklore. Folktales are also often made of combinations of plots, and this too is a feature of Esther in which some scholars have claimed to identify more than one 'source' story, while others have insisted that the work as a whole is a unity. The book is keenly interested in perennially popular topics such as the exercise of authority, and the behaviour of women and foreigners, and it champions the trickster and underdog as it promotes an ironic form of justice. The characteristics which made Talmon allocate Esther to the wisdom tradition could very well locate it in the folk tradition instead. Readers who wish to pursue the comparison will find that many of the motifs used in Esther (the banished wife, the foolish king) feature in Thompson's Motif Index of folklore. It will be noticed that the more one inclines to see Esther as folklore, the less probable it appears that the book is history. Scholarship need not doom itself, says Brenner, to look for this 'mirror kingdom'.

Internal Structure and Literary Techniques

In a phase of scholarly criticism now drawing to a close, the study of any biblical text as literature was in fact done with an eye to historical matters. An *a priori* assumption was made that the text could be analysed into portions stemming from different hands (identifiable on grounds of internal consistency) and/or segments of oral tradition (which can be recognized because they take on a range of characteristic forms), the whole being put together by a redactor—or perhaps a sequence of redactors. In this way, the pre-history of the received text could be reconstructed and each element allocated to its most likely historical setting. This type of scholarship, which has been dominant for at least a century, is losing its hegemony for two main reasons, one positive and the other negative. The negative reason is that its favoured tools (source criticism, form criticism and redaction criticism) are now seen to be methodologically flawed: partly incompatible and by no means 'objective' in that scholars of equal integrity and competence could and did apply the methods and reach widely divergent conclusions. The positive reason is that insofar as historical criticism does produce results which command a wide degree of acceptance its task is largely complete. Scholarship can move on to apply new tools to its task—principally tools which study how texts function as wholes in their present form, tools which can produce refreshing insights that cut across the findings of historical criticism but are of course no more 'objective'. Modern scholarship has made the fundamental discovery that 'objectivity' is something of a chimera.

This change is readily apparent in Esther scholarship. Historical criticism had already by the beginning of this century cast doubt on the historicity of the tale, but the analytical and excavative method can of course equally be applied to the illumination of the pre-history of a text which is not historical. Indeed, the quest to uncover the stages by which the Esther tradition grew is, as explained in Chapter 9 above, very much a live area of study, dominated by Clines and more recently widened by Milik, Day and others. This discussion is unusual in that it is as much or more interested in stages of the Esther tradition which post-date the Masoretic text as it is in the stages that predate it. But here it is the possibility of applying source and redaction criticism to the Masoretic text that will first concern us.

Two significant scholars in this field are Cazelles and Bardtke. Cazelles, noting that a prominent feature of Esther is its 'twoness' (two lists of the king's servants [1.10, 14]; two references to assembling the women [2.8, 19]; two consultations between Haman and his wife and friends [5.14; 6.13]; two unsummoned appearances by Esther before the king [5.2; 8.3]; two accounts of the deaths of Haman's sons [9.6-10, 13-14]; two fasts [4.1-3, 16]; two feasts hosted by Ahasuerus in ch. 1 and two by Esther in 5.5 and 7.1; all leading up to two days for the festival of Purim!) suggested that Esther is a conflation of two stories. One could be a 'liturgical' text drawing upon a bacchanalian Persian new year festival and centring around Esther and the people of the Persian provinces, while the other could be more 'historical', centring on Mordecai and on intrigues at court having to do with a persecution of the Jews of Susa.

A variant of this theory, suggested by Bardtke, is essentially that there were three stories, two being much as described by Cazelles and the third being the brief story of Vashti the deposed Persian queen, which perhaps began as an apocryphal harem tale. Bardtke suggested that the author of Esther had all these stories at his disposal in some lost Jewish midrashic collection, and innocently combined them by identifying Esther with Mordecai's niece (named as 'Hadassah, that is Esther' in 2.7).

The evidence of 'twoness' is undeniable, and it is odd that the book has one bad character but two good ones. Nevertheless, it is fair to object as Berg does that the 'seams' in Esther are not all that visible; even the Vashti story, which at first sight seems easily detachable from the rest, is essential to the whole story because it explains how Esther, a lowly Jewess, came to be queen at all, and gives some indication of how dangerous it will be for her ever to disobey Ahasuerus. The other supposedly separate stories are even more difficult to separate or reconstruct, and it is noteworthy that even Clines, who of course does doubt that the MT of Esther is an authorial unity confines his suspicions to the material in chs. 9 and 10.

Another proponent of historical criticism who should be specially mentioned is Dommershausen, who has done the most careful form-critical work on Esther, labelling all the components in turn (e.g. Est. 1 'narration'; 2.1-4 'servant speech'; 2.5-7 'biographical note' and so on) and examining the precise ways in which the literary techniques used vary from the Esther norm and thus magnify the effect of key scenes in the story. Dommershausen's work is a good illustration of the fact that historical criticism at its best does pay faithful attention to the literary features of the text under study and indeed is founded on them. But he has also been criticized (Berg) for displaying the weakness of historical criticism, namely that he has failed to see how each of his 'forms' is influenced by its context and thus to appreciate fully how the book pulls together as a whole, as a complete short story.

The most schematic understanding of the structure of Esther is that of Radday (1973) who suggested a chiastic scheme, but this is oversimplified.

How does the story function as a whole? Alter describes biblical narrative as containing elaborately integrated systems of repetition in a scale ascending from the leitwort to the motif to the theme (an idea which is part of the value system of the narrative), and finally to the sequence of action; the last three of these are 'significant structuring principles in Esther' (Fox).

On the broadest level, Esther is a classic linear tale with a beginning (1.1–2.23), middle (3.1–9.19) and end (9.20–10.3), separated not only by distinctive subject matter but also by chronological gaps. The first phase is leisurely, taking some six years, the second more stressful, taking place within a year (and much of the key action within eighteen days), and the third has broadened out into the continuing time in which the festival of Purim is celebrated regularly. As to its theme, Esther has been described as a 'politico-philosophical guide to life and survival' (so Brenner in the *Companion to Esther*), dealing particularly with how the powerless can achieve their goals, and with the inversion of fate; it can also be seen as meditating on the nature of law.

On the next level, there are several important structuring devices. One is the recurrence of the motif of feasting: Esther has twenty of the forty-six occurrences of *mišteh* in the Hebrew Bible, and feasting is the dominant motif of Purim itself. Feasts, of which there are ten in all (and the subsidiary motif of fasts) are important occasions for bringing out the irony of the tale, as characters gain and lose power. They may also emphasize the honour and wealth of the main protagonists, not only Ahasuerus at the beginning, but also by implication the Jewish community feasting at Purim at the end, with Mordecai (a Saulide) arguably presiding as king. On the basis that the feasting motif appears in the very first chapter, in the twofold form that will be reflected in the two-day observance of Purim at the end of the book, Berg argues that the whole book does lead up to the institution of Purim, a connection some have denied, although she admits that it is not clear that the original narrator knew the festival by that name.

Reversal is also a major structuring device, especially in the section from Esther 3–8 inclusive. Fox and Berg have independently argued for a series of 'theses' and 'antitheses' which mirror each other in the book, and Berg believes that the turning point comes with the end of the 'theses' in 4.13-14 (between the two fasts, the two royal edicts, and the main pairs of banquets) and the start of the 'antitheses', although Fox locates it at 6.10 between Esther's two banquets, the point at which the actions begin to make good the reversals hinted at in the unfolding of the story. The author has made highly effective use of *peripety*, defined by Aristotle in his *Poetics* as an action or state of affairs producing the opposite of the intended result. Brenner (*Companion to Esther*) has not only explored the way in which symmetries and repetitions mirror the 'inversion of fate' theme but also categorizes (pp. 72-73) a set of eleven duplication and multiplication techniques used in Esther. None of these is unique to Esther but their cumulative weight is 'quite exceptional' and surely forms part of the message of the book, as well as its medium.

For Berg, kingship is a dominant motif in its own right. The *mlk* root which stands behind the words for 'king' 'queen' and 'rule' occurs over 250 times in 167 verses. (Repetition is Esther's most characteristic literary weakness, which is why the Greek translator found it possible to 'fillet' the book.) Berg speculates that the Purim feasts were hosted by royalty and that this was part of their nationalistic attraction.

Related to the kingship motif is that of obedience and disobedience. It is noticeable that only the Jews are rewarded for the latter. Unlike Vashti, Esther appears before the king when she wishes to (5.1), and even makes the king appear at her banquets, twice! The obedience/disobedience motif hints at an important function of the Esther story in a community living in circumstances never envisaged by the Torah. (*dāt*, the word used for law in Esther, is only otherwise found in Deut. 33.2 and Ezra 8.36). Not even the Law, it seems, takes precedence over the community's welfare. Jewish identity may be dangerous to the holder and may demand self-sacrifice of them, so that mutual loyalty—which does not exclude loyalty to the foreign power—is of paramount importance. The author is convinced that loyalty to both the temporal ruler and to Judaism is possible in an alien state, and indeed essential in that the future of Judaism is largely bound up with the future of diaspora Jews.

It is even possible that the way in which the many coincidences that are a feature of Esther occur in connection with peripety is intended to convey the subliminal message that the Jews are meant by God to be inviolable (Berg). This is a controversial point for two reasons. First, one message of the book is probably that humans have to make a 'correct' response to history, if history despite its expected course is to 'radically realign itself in a favourable direction'. Berg herself is aware of this. More seriously, it contains the danger of a false 'divine right' theology—or more properly an ideology. These are both reasons that could explain why the author has been so reluctant to mention God (even when it is difficult to avoid doing so, as in 4.14 and the fasting scenes). From the standpoint of Judaism, this does not mean that the book believes in blind fate rather than the providence of God, but it does mean that God's providence is veiled in everyday life; the book stops short, however, of claiming overtly that the Jews have a special place in the divine purpose. Its partial secularity is deliberate (Fox).

It remains to consider the role of characterization in forming the theology of Esther. A new departure here has been made by Fox who devotes much of the second half of his commentary volume to studies of Vashti, Xerxes, Haman, Mordecai, Esther, the Jews collectively, God (despite his never being mentioned) and the World. This is a direct counterposition to that of Moore, who stated that the major characters in Esther are 'so superficially drawn that it is difficult to identify very long or intensively with either the book's villains or heroes'.

It is, however, very instructive to see how Fox's surveys of previous responses to these supposedly cardboard characters reveal a great range of responses, as readers project their own thoughts into the silences. Paradoxically, the flattest character emerges as that of Mordecai, whose behaviour is always direct, shows no development, but is ultimately opaque. The others, though sketchily drawn, function as effectively and suggestively as the characters in a fairy-tale.

Work on the relative literary characteristics of the versions is also well under way. The complexity of this task, already hinted at in the discussion in Chapter 9 above on the identification of social contexts for each of the versions, is underlined by the fact that two case studies by Kristin de Troyer on Est. 2.8-18 and Timothy Beal on Esther 1 (both in the *Companion to Esther*), reach opposite conclusions as to the 'gender' of the A and B texts, De Troyer finding that the Masoretic text and the A-text are covertly male, but that the B-text softens the bias; Beal finding the Masoretic text's sympathy for Vashti to have trace effects over the whole book. This difference of opinion no doubt reflects the difficulty of attempting to 'gender' texts, that is, to ascertain whether they reflect or promote characteristically male or female concerns, at all.

However, Day's comparative study of the characterization of Esther in all three of the major versions raises different concerns, offering both a suggested methodology for the assessment of character (*Three Faces of a Queen*, pp. 24-25) in literature, and some observations on the implications of the three very different Esthers that emerge. Day wishes to argue that it is the Esther story in essence that is or should be canonical, not a particular version, so that all the Esthers should be equally valid concerns for feminist criticism. The versions should be viewed as extensions of the well-known inner-biblical phenomenon of providing doublets or other multiples of its material (culminating in the provision of four Gospels). Each has different insights to offer, and those which do not happen to be in the Bible may sometimes prove to contain 'more original or otherwise preferable' material. It will be evident that this raises very large questions which may be easier to resolve in the case of Esther (in which Protestant and Catholic traditions happen to have favoured different versions) than in the case of other books, but it is a question that may spread into the interpretation of other biblical books in the next phase of biblical study, reflecting the modern view that the Bible is not so much an authoritative source as an invaluable resource.

For Further Reading

S.B. Berg, *The Book of Esther. Motifs, Themes, Structures* (SBLDS, 44; Chico, CA: Scholars Press, 1979).

E. Bickermann, *Four Strange Books of the Bible: Jonah, Daniel, Koheleth, Esther* (New York: Schocken Books, 1967), pp. 171-240.

H. Cazelles, 'Note sur la composition du rouleau d'Esther', in H. Gros and F. Mussner (eds.), *Lex tua veritas: Festschrift für Hubert Junker* (Trier: Paulinus Verlag, 1961), pp. 17-29 (= Moore, *Studies*, pp. 424-36).

D.J.A. Clines, Ezra, *Nehemiah, Esther* (NCB; Grand Rapids: Eerdmans, 1984).

—'Reading Esther from Left to Right: Contemporary Strategies for Reading a Biblical Text', in D.J.A. Clines, S.E. Fowl and S.E. Porter (eds.), *The Bible in Three Dimensions. Essays in Celebration of the Fortieth Anniversary of the Department of Biblical Studies, University of Sheffield* (Sheffield: JSOT Press, 1990), pp. 31-52.

N.L. Collins, 'Did Esther Fast on the 15th Nisan? An Extended Comment on Esther 3.12', *RB* 100 (1993), pp. 533-61. (On the parallels between the stories of Esther and the Exodus).

W. Dommershausen, *Die Estherrolle. Stil und Ziel einer alttestamentlichen Schrift* (SBM, 6; Stuttgart: Katholisches Bibelwerk, 1968), pp. 5-174.

M.V. Fox, *Character and Ideology in the Book of Esther* (Studies in Personalities of the Old Testament; Columbia, SC: University of South Carolina, 1991).

—'The Redaction of the Books of Esther. On Reading Composite Texts', *Bib* 75 (1994), pp. 106-12.

R. Gordis, 'Religion, Wisdom and History in the Book of Esther. A New Solution to an Ancient Crux', *JBL* 100 (1981), pp. 359-88.

W.L. Humphreys, 'A Life-style for Diaspora: A Study of the Tales of Esther and Daniel', *JBL* 92 (1973), pp. 211-23.

A. Lacocque, 'Haman in the Book of Esther', *HAR* 11 (1987), pp. 207-22.

A. Meinhold, 'Die Gattung der Josephsgeschichte und des Estherbuches. Diasporanovelle II', *ZAW* 88 (1976), pp. 7-93.

—'Zu Aufbau und Mitte des Estherbuches', *VT* 33 (1988), pp. 435-45.

Y. Radday, 'Chiasam in Joshua, Judges and Others', *Linguistica Biblica* 3 (1973), pp. 6-13.

S. Talmon, '"Wisdom" in the Book of Esther', *VT* 13 (1963), pp. 419-55.

S. Thompson, *The Motif-Index of Folk-Literature* (Bloomington: Indiana University Press, 1955–58).

L.M. Wills, *The Jew in the Court of the Foreign King: Ancient Jewish Court Legends* (Minneapolis: Fortress Press, 1990), pp. 153-91.

Indexes

Index of References

Index of Authors